Loving Someone Behind Bars

by

Hilda Miller-Jones
with poems and commentary by Frederick Jones

McDougal & Associates is an organization dedicated
to spreading the Gospel of the Lord Jesus Christ to as
many people as possible in the shortest time possible.

Published by:

McDougal & Associates
18896 Greenwell Springs Road
Greenwell Springs, LA 70739

www.thepublishedword.com

ISBN: 978-1-940461-96-0

Printed in the U.S., the U.K. and Australia
For Worldwide Distribution

For with God

nothing shall be

impossible.

Luke 1:37

Dedication

This book is dedicated, first and foremost, to God. Without Him, I am nothing.

> *Father God, in the name of Jesus, I thank You for the years of your divine Spirit leading and guiding me on this walk of encouraging Your people. I am grateful for the knowledge that You are a Keeper and You keep those who are committed to you.*

Without God, this book would have never been written.

> *Thank You, Lord, for Your love and guidance through my experiences in this book. I couldn't have succeeded without You.*

> *With God, all things are possible.*
> Matthew 19:26

My sincerest thanks to the late Dr. Rev. Josie Phillips. Her vision and energies influenced me to write this book. She was indeed a tribute to the Kingdom of God.

I wish to honor the prophet of God, Prophet Samuel Green, Remnant Church Kingdom Ministries, a man of God who prophesied this book and its impact on women with incarcerated spouses.

To Pastor Dwayne Coleman, Pastor of the Church of God in Zachary, Louisiana, from 1999 to 2012. God touched his heart in 1999 to open the door and allow us to hold services for inmates. Those services continue to the present. Faith Hope Love Ministry holds a bimonthly service at the Louisiana State Police Barracks, to help encourage inmates, by preaching and teaching the Gospel of Jesus Christ. I am so grateful to God for touching this man's heart.

To Pastor Vivian Collins: She brought me the final step by introducing me to her publisher.

To Frederick Jones, aka Ricky, poet, inspirational writer, composer, musician, best friend and brother in the Lord, for dedicating his love, patience and, although I sometimes rebelled, his constructive criticism for me, the twins and my goals. Through a family member, his sudden appearance in my life has been a breath of fresh air for both of us. It was he who gave me the name Reverend Lady.

Contents

Book 1

Love Conquers All

Why I Wrote This Book

Luke 1:37

For with God nothing shall be impossible.

There are consequences for loving someone behind bars. If you choose to do it, don't be controlled by the circumstance. Instead, you must be in control of the circumstances. I wrote this book because I myself made that choice, to love someone behind bars, and I had to face the significant consequences.

Introduction

1 Corinthians 13:13
And now abideth faith, hope, charity [love],
these three; but the greatest of these is charity.

The year 1998/1999 was the first year of re-uniting with Hank, and it was a year filled with joy and excitement. If loving him was wrong, I didn't want to be right. I loved him, and I wanted the world to know that I loved him. It had taken me more than thirty years to realize what I had been looking for and that I'd had it all along. I was just in the wrong place at the right time.

The man I was in love with was an inmate, but I still wanted the world to know about it. The emptiness and void I had experienced for so long were now gone. Hank's love filled up my life.

That should not be surprising. The Bible states that everything but love will fail. It was because of Jesus' love that I could forgive the past and love again. And that is my story.

Hilda Miller-Jones

Chapter 1

Seasons of Change

Ecclesiastes 3:1

To every thing there is a season, and a time to every purpose under the heaven.

I can't remember a time that I didn't pray. Even in my Christless years, in my own innocent way, I did my best to speak with God. I didn't understand much of what I was doing; I just tried to pray to the God of my elders.

I suppose now that my prayers were more like wishes, for I didn't have much faith in the blessing of them. Oh, but once God blessed me, I knew it was He. Only God is able to do certain things. Praise His name!

When I did begin to pray correctly, I prayed with sincerity and energy, and I have never once stopped praying. Praise God! But allow me to go back and tell you more about how it all happened.

I was raised in the small town of Braithwaite, Louisiana, and lived with my mother's sister,

Aunt Joyce, her husband, Uncle Pat, and their ten children. Mom lived and worked in New Orleans, and my dad was never part of my life.

In those days, there was only one school in the Braithwaite area, and that school was in nearby Phoenix, Louisiana. Henry "Hank" Miller and I were students there together in the third grade, and we became friends and then childhood sweethearts. It was all very innocent and beautiful, and I held on to the memory of it for a very long time.

At the age of thirteen, I relocated to the city to live with my mom. The transition wasn't nearly as pleasant as I had imagined. Leaving what had become, for me, my family and also my friends and starting all over again wasn't easy at all. Nevertheless, it seemed like time for a change.

What a change it proved to be! I changed from country life to city life. I started attending a new school. I lost touch with most of my friends and had to make new ones. One of the friends I found in New Orleans over time was a boy named Anthony.

Anthony was employed by Lionel's Record Company, and after school he would pass by our place selling records. The two of us became good friends. Then, after only a few months of being friends, our relationship became serious, and he asked my mom if he could marry me. My nosey step-dad asked Anthony if he *wanted* to get married or we *had* to get married. Anthony answered, "Both. We *want* to get married, and we *have* to get married."

I was eighteen at the time, Anthony and I got married, and in short order I gave birth to three children, two girls (one of our twin daughters was stillborn) and a boy. Then, during the eight month of my pregnancy with our fourth child, Anthony tragically passed away.

We were at a family gathering on Lake Pontchartrain that day, and Anthony decided to go swimming and drowned. His sudden death left our children without a father and me without a husband. Needless to say, life suddenly became very complicated for us all.

Chapter 2

The Joy of Finding Love Again

Song of Solomon 3:1-2

By night on my bed I sought him whom my soul loveth: I sought him, but I found him not. I will rise now, and go about the city in the streets, and in the broad ways I will seek him whom my soul loveth: I sought him, but I found him not.

We somehow got through those years, and I was able to secure a part-time job to help support us. Every weekend I would go to visit Aunt Joyce and Uncle Pat. It was the only place I could get a reliable free-of-charge baby-sitter and be able to get out and do something without the children.

One Sunday afternoon, I decided to go out and have a drink or two before returning home, and I ran into Hank, my childhood memory. We danced and drank and decided we still liked each other's company. We were both single and unattached.

After I had moved to New Orleans, Hank had joined the Marines and done a stint of military service. Now he was back, and I was back, and we were both happy about it.

In fact, we were suddenly caught up in the moment of seeing one another again after so long. Hank had turned out well, I thought, and he thought the same about me. Of course, as we gazed into each other's eyes, we had nothing but outward appearances to enlighten us. We couldn't see beyond that.

The main thought I had was that this man of my childhood puppy loves was single, and so was I, and that he would make a good husband, a good father and a good provider, and that was just what I needed. Suddenly we felt like two people in love, two people who had been lost in the folds of life and hadn't seen each other since childhood but who had now been reunited by a God we knew very little about. In that moment, I felt so blessed:

Hank was handsome and well-built, a lady's man indeed, and I decided that *in my life* was where he needed to be. He was *my* blessing. I immediately overlooked every minor obstacle—having to travel to and from my job, spending hours away from home and whatever my family members would think about it all. None of that mattered now. I was floating on Cloud Nine and did not want to come down.

I was in love, but the clock was ticking. There was music in my ears, but the clock was ticking. In his arms, I was feeling something I hadn't experienced in a very long while, but the clock was ticking. Memories of our third-grade puppy love and its re-connection kept us smiling.

Only scratching the surface, I began to ponder the longevity of our new-born relationship, refusing to allow my joy to be taken away. As adults, we had an opportunity to enjoy one another, and the upsides seemed to be great. But, for some reason, I began to question myself: Was this just a transient fling? Or did Hank and I have a future together? Would we be able to live up to each other's expectations? I didn't know. Neither of us knew what the future held, but it appeared that we were both willing to give it a try.

As Whitney Houston sang:

I have nothing,
I didn't want to hurt anymore,
I couldn't let him walk away.

Hank was breaking down the walls of loneliness in my life, and suddenly I was convinced that he was the remedy for what ailed me.

Psalm 18:6

In my distress I called upon the LORD, and cried unto my God: he heard my voice out of his temple, and my cry came before him, even into his ears.

We quickly decided that this would not be our last time seeing each other. "Try me," Hank pleaded. "You need you. Try me! Try me! And, my love, I will always be true. Oh, I need you."

I was not hard to convince. It was a new beginning for me. I now had a love of my own, a love I didn't have to hide. That one night had changed my life dramatically.

Returning to work the next day was difficult because the memories of the night before were fresh. Then, after a few weeks, other than our weekend visits, life became a drudgery for me.

I so wanted to be with Hank and also with my kids, but my travel time back and forth to work became an issue. I spent way too much time on the road, and that created a problem.

Still, those weekend visits seemed like the best solution for us because of the children's school and my job. But, once the weekends were over, it was a very sad time for me. I wanted Hank to make my weeping heart smile. I wanted his love, and I was willing to earn it.

In time, Hank and I had a child, a daughter and things reached the point that I no longer wanted to return to the city. I needed to be with my man. The commute back and forth, traveling down those lonely, dark roads, along with my need to be at home with him, had taken its toll. Supposedly out of concern for my safety (traveling alone) and my being away too much, Hank, finally insisted that I quit my job and move in with him.

It was an easy decision for me to make. That same night, the kids and I left the city. The struggle was finally over, and I was glad about it. Of course, I never revealed to Hank that it had been an answer to prayer. My innocent faith and prayers had unlocked the door to a blessing. Yes, this was exciting! It was my first knowledgeable sign of God's love for me.

In any relationship, you must weigh the entire situation. I was far too easily satisfied with simple comforts and conveniences and couldn't see the forest for the trees. I actually imagined that Hank and I would never have another problem.

In the beginning, Hank and I isolated ourselves. We were confined in our own little world. It was as if no one else existed. Hank became my god, and I was his possession.

In my foolish way of thinking, I convinced myself that everything was wonderful and would continue to be wonderful. After all, I had a provider, a husband and a father for my kids. What else did I need?

Philippians 4:6

Be careful for nothing; but in every thing by prayer and supplication with thanksgiving let your requests be made known unto God.

Jeremiah 17:5

Thus saith the LORD; Cursed be the man that trusteth in man, and maketh flesh his arm, and whose heart departeth from the LORD.

In time, Hank and I got married. Other than the couple who witnessed the ceremony, no one knew about our union. But when I became Hank's wife, it brought me an unexplainable joy. Words cannot describe the moment. A change had come over me, a wonderful change. My life was finally complete. Hank was my everything. I was happy, but in the mist of my happiness, there was no God, and that could only spell trouble for our future.

Chapter 3

A Better Life and What It Meant

Hebrews 13:4

Marriage is honourable in all, and the bed undefiled: but whoremongers and adulterers God will judge.

When I shared the news of Hank and I getting married with my family, they all thought I had made a wrong decision. They were sure marrying Hank was a mistake, but I refused to hear it. None of what they said mattered to me. I now had an opportunity for a better life for me and my children, and I didn't want anything to spoil it.

Then, only a month after we were married, Hank's house suddenly became entirely too small. We talked about it, and he said he didn't want to rent anymore. He wanted to be a homeowner. We also talked about the advantages of being in the city, so we bought a house in New Orleans.

That first year of my marriage to Hank was awesome. We had our own home in a quiet neighborhood, and things were great. Purchasing a home had been the right decision. Hank had gotten a better-paying job, bought us a car, and life was wonderful. He was everything I had imagined and more. Little did I know that the clock was still ticking, but I was in Seventh Heaven.

At Mardi-Gras time, I was on the head float in the parade, celebrating the end of hard times. I was totally unaware of that ticking clock. In a brief period, we had accomplished a lot. We were in our mid-twenties and doing better than most couples we knew. At least, that's how I saw it. I was in the world and keeping up with the Joneses. (Ironically, now, I am a Jones).

Unfortunately, during that period of joys and comforts, I did not acknowledge Jesus, the One who had made it all possible. It was Jesus who had looked beyond my faults and saw a need to bless me. Hank and I were caught up with the worldly order of life, and, for us, God didn't even exist.

We didn't go to church, didn't even think about giving God thanks for pouring His many blessings into our lives. God continuously blessed us, but it was certainly not because we were deserving of His blessings.

We did not pay tithes on the money we earned or give love offerings to any church. God has said:

1 Thessalonians 5:18

In every thing give thanks: for this is the will of God in Christ Jesus concerning you.

Any relationship is challenging. To have a relationship, one must be willing to bend. In a relationship with God, you must be the one to bend and allow God to become the centerpiece of your life. That we had not done.

God's Word speaks to marriage partners:

Ephesians 5:22-24

Wives, submit yourselves unto your own husbands, as unto the Lord. For the husband is the head of the wife, even as Christ is the head of the church: and he is the saviour of the body. Therefore as the church is subject

unto Christ, so let the wives be to their own
husbands in every thing.

Ephesians 5:25 and 28
*Husbands, love your wives, even as Christ
also loved the church, and gave himself for it.
So ought men to love their wives as their
own bodies. He that loveth his wife loveth
himself.*

As might have been predicted, eventually, the
once-flaming embers of the love between Hank
and me dimmed, and we began to drift apart. Before long, he was seldom home. When he stayed
away like that, I allowed myself to become lonely
and depressed. I even considered suicide at one
point. My emotional downward spiral brought
hopelessness on every occasion.

Our marriage was failing, and, for me, failure was not an option. It was either do or die.
My family, of course, now said, "I told you it
wouldn't work." And what could I say? It would
have worked if Hank and I had let God have His
proper place in our marriage.

I tried very hard toward the end to show Hank
love, but he didn't want it. It is a proven fact

that a wife is usually the last to know when her husband is cheating on her. Many of us have depended on love to help us overcome any marital inadequacies. Before long I learned that when Hank had gone out, supposedly to walk the dog, he was actually visiting a lady friend just a block from our home. I had seen lipstick on his shirt, so I should have known. Somehow I didn't want to believe the truth.

Love makes us do foolish things. Hank and I had been young, and our love had no real long-term value in our lives. But now that our marriage was failing, I didn't want to desert the relationship without giving it another chance to flourish. I tried to be patient and understanding, but things quickly went from bad to worse. Behind layers and layers of heartache and tears, love was unable to manifest itself, and soon we were a couple sharing a senseless dependency for one another. We were both miserable.

Love is a process. It's sort of like planting a rose bush. We water it, it gets a little sunshine, and in time, we prune it, and the results are beautiful roses. Because of our worldly living, Hank and I were a pair of wilted roses. Instead of reaping the fruits of a holy union, we were reaping the fruits of our worldliness and godlessness.

We no longer produced beautiful flowers. That same planting and growing process should have been applied to our relationship, but it wasn't, and we had no one to blame but ourselves. Hank and I were the guilty parties in this case. We had not allowed our relationship to flourish because we had been so preoccupied with what the world offered us. Love, therefore, was not given a fair chance.

At first, it was his anger, his moodiness, his staying out all night and cheating on me. Then, after a while, I just gave up. In my heart, I knew that I should have tried harder, but somehow I just didn't have it in me.

1 Corinthians 13:4

> *Charity suffereth long, and is kind; charity envieth not; charity vaunteth not itself, is not puffed up.*

Eventually Hank took the decision to file for divorce. He signed the papers so that I could keep our home, but I had to give up his last name. (Ironically, again, my family name is now Miller-Jones).

Chapter 4

The Unthinkable Happened

Proverbs 13:15
Good understanding giveth favour: but the way of transgressors is hard.

Then, suddenly, the unthinkable happened. Just thirty days after our divorce was finalized, Hank was suddenly featured on the nightly news. He had been accused of taking someone's life. The news reporter stated that a sixteen-year-old boy had thrown a frisbee and hit Hank's car, and Hank had shot him. Tragically, the boy died en route to the hospital.

The next morning, Hank turned himself in. I went to visit him, but he insisted that I go on with my life. He was soon put on trial and sentenced to fifty years to life. He was just twenty-five years old at the time.

My children loved Hank and kept in contact with him in prison, but I decided that he was right. I needed to move on with my life. After a few years, he wrote to me, but I didn't answer. He kept writing from time to time, eventually asking me to send him some clothing. I was determined not to get caught up in all of that. But Hank didn't give up easily. He kept writing.

About that time, I began seeking Jesus. A friend had invited me to attend a Saturday morning prayer service, and I found it to be very encouraging. I soon realized that not only did Hank need Jesus; so did I.

I met a group of Holy-Ghost-filled women who told me wonderful things about Jesus. I surely needed this Jesus. In 1978, I finally accepted the Lord as my personal Savior and started holding prayer services in my home.

John 3:3

> *Verily, verily unto thee. Except a man be born again he cannot see the kingdom of God.*

John 3:16

> *For God so loved the world, that he gave his only begotten Son, that whosoever believeth in him should not perish, but have everlasting life.*

I now had a strong desire for a new beginning, including a new husband. The leader of the group, however, told me that God would restore my marriage. She also told me that, in the meantime, I had to abstain from sexual relations with any other man.

"Abstain?" What was that?

Fornication was another thing she warned me about. All of that was new to me. I never went back to that group because I didn't want to hear it. And I certainly did not want to be married to someone who was in prison. That was the furthest thing from my mind.

But life was hard for a single mom with four kids, and it was not getting any easier. I was looking for love in all the wrong places and not finding anything truly satisfying.

Roman 6:23

> *For the wages of sin is death, but the gift of God is eternal life in Christ Jesus our Lord.*

Why didn't I want to be reunited with Hank? Hank had served in the Marines, and they had taught him how to fight and kill and how to always be on guard, but they had failed to prepare him for civilian life. He was always on guard, even with me. So I had to learn to always be on guard with him. After he had been honorably discharged, he had brought home with him a lingering edginess. His military training, in obsessive ways, remained a basic part of his everyday life.

I had believed in my heart that Hank wanted the best for me and the children, but he just wasn't stable. He had set many family rules, and he expected us to follow them all. Sometimes it was as if we were *all* in the Marines.

We had both been so young and foolish, and neither of us had known the true meaning of love. We both wanted happiness and love, but God somehow hadn't been in the equation. Now I cried out to God, and He heard me. Oh yes, He heard me.

Hank was not the only guilty party. When he went astray, I followed suit. At first, I tried to do my best. I really did. But that had its limits. With him, it was, first, the anger and then the cheating, and then I tried to make him pay for hurting me so much.

Could I somehow forgive him and start over? That was not in my thinking. He had done too many things contrary to his marriage vows. He had hurt me one time too many.

John 15:7

If ye abide in me, and my words abide in you, ye shall ask what ye will, and it shall be done unto you.

Without Jesus in the center of your life, your travels will be filled with turmoil without relief. Prayer is always the key. In the beginning, I felt the need to pray. The reality was that I was still in the process of learning to pray. Hank never felt that need. But without Jesus you can do nothing, and that described the two of us.

Chapter 5

The Joy of Reuniting

Hebrews 11:1

Now faith is a substances of things hoped for, the evidence of things not seen.

As you know from the introduction to the book, we did get together again. The first year of reuniting was filled with joy and excitement. At that moment, "If loving him was wrong I didn't want to be right." The man I was in love with was in prison, and I didn't care who knew it. He was many miles away, but that didn't matter at all.

How did this come about? Well, after serving half of his sentence, Hank was transferred out of the infamous Angola Prison and began trying to contact me again. Even though twenty years had gone by, he would write and call on a weekly basis. For the longest time, I never replied or accepted those calls.

Then Hank called on a day I had just ended a complicated relationship with a married man. I wanted more out of life and had set new goals for myself, and a married man was not included.

My first goal now was to stop drinking. Along my travels I had began drinking way too much. I had been heavily into the party life, but now I was tired of the way I was living. I was miserable. Falling on my knees, I asked God to forgive me for my sins. I asked Him to take the taste for alcohol out of my mouth. I knew that God was not pleased with the way I was living, and I asked him to straighten me out.

In the meantime, as I noted earlier, Hank and the children had kept in contact. That was his way of keeping tabs on me. I was, by then, one of the lead operators at a well-known facility in New Orleans, and one day Hank called my job asking for me. He was telling everyone he was my husband. I told my supervisor that I didn't have a husband.

But the calls did not stop. Hank kept calling, and I kept denying that I even knew him. I finally admitted to the supervisor that he was my ex-husband. She accepted the call herself and asked him not to call there anymore. Did that stop Hank? Oh, no! Not in the least. He was determined!

Matthew 26:34-35

> *Jesus said unto him, Verily I say unto thee,*
> *That this night, before the cock crow, thou*
> *shalt deny me thrice.*
> *Peter said unto him, Though I should die*
> *with thee, yet will I not deny thee. Likewise*
> *also said all the disciples.*

Peter said that he, among all men, would not be offended because of Jesus, but the Lord knew the heart of every man. He knew my heart too.

The idea of me speaking to Hank wasn't all that bad. I just didn't want my co-workers to know he was connected to me. I was afraid of what they might say if they knew I was once married to a man who was now a prison inmate. I felt that such knowledge would ruin my reputation, and for that reason, I avoided direct contact with him.

But my avoidance didn't stop Hank. He continuously found ways to try to contact me. Soon other operators began passing remarks to me, "Oh, that Mr. Miller is so nice and polite! Girl, you should talk to him." I finally gave in and accepted one of Hank's calls. Without hesitation, he asked me to come and visit him. He hadn't even asked how I was doing.

I started laughing. Hank was still Hank! "Why not?" I answered. The problem was that my feelings for him, that had long been sleeping peacefully, suddenly yawned and began to stir themselves.

The children had been constantly trying to convince me of Hank's miraculous change. When I told them of my decision to visit him in prison, they were more than pleased.

After all those years, I didn't know what to expect once Hank and I were face to face. Oh, but one thing was for sure: I was going to see Hank Miller again, and I was very excited.

Matthew 6:14-15

For if ye forgive men their trespasses, your heavenly Father will also forgive you: but if ye forgive not men their trespasses, neither will your Father forgive your trespasses.

Arriving at the prison barracks, I felt lost and scared. Then, Hank approached me, just as neat and calm as he could be and looking like he didn't have a care in the world. He took me by the arm and escorted me to a picnic area where visiting family members were allowed to spend time with their loved ones.

Soon we were seated next to each other, and I stared into Hank's face. He looked so different. I asked myself, "Is this man really a prisoner?" He looked so good.

Hank was dressed in jeans, shirt and boots and was looking better than some of the guys I had seen walking down Canal Street recently. And, as always, he was very charming. The children and I spent the entire day with him. We barbecued, laughed about the old days and enjoyed the time together as a family.

It was obvious that Hank and I were glad to see each other. In fact, the end of the day came too fast for all of us, and I didn't want to leave. But there was no choice, only the hope of seeing Hank again. He begged me to come back, and I agreed to return for another visit—the following week.

Before the kids and I departed that day, Hank told all the other inmates that his family had finally come to see about him and introduced me to everyone as his wife. He had me hooked once again. And now visiting Hank in prison became a weekly endeavor that somehow consumed me.

For the first time in a long time, I was very happy. As I was driving home, I heard a voice saying, "Henry needs you." I can't explain it, but I wanted to be needed by someone. I liked that idea.

The next week, the night before I was scheduled to visit Hank, I had a visit from my ex (the married man). His charming words and request for one last drink for old times sake brought back too many old memories and I consented.

But that was a big mistake! The next morning, I was scheduled to visit Hank, but I couldn't even look him in the eyes. He noticed immediately and asked, "What's wrong?"

I told him I had run into my ex.

He said, "That shouldn't have been a problem."

He knew, but he pretended not to, and I was left with a sense of overwhelming guilt.

While I was drowning in my sorrows, Hank was making plans for our future. He was persistent. He called me every day, both at work and at home. Our personal phone bill quickly exceeded a thousand dollars a month. How did that get paid? Hank knew how to accumulate funds. He did hobby crafts in prison, and it brought in a lot of money.

Now he not only wanted his freedom; it appeared that the kids and I were a major part of his plans for the future. He began showering me with gifts. All eyes were on me, and I was on Cloud Nine again.

I didn't have a car at the time, and Hank provided the funds for me to get one. He was an inmate, but he was also very resourceful.

Next Hank advised me that he was planning to go before the Parole Board and needed me to go with him. I was ignorant of how the penal system's Parole Board worked. It wasn't as simple as I had imagined.

He also asked me, for the second time, to marry him. He said that if we were married, it would increase his chances of making parole.

Psalm 34:4

I sought the Lord, and he heard me and delivered me from all my fears.

After I had been visiting Hank for almost a year, we were re-married. He had told his mother we were getting married in August, and she said, "Not a good month to marry." So we changed our wedding date to September 2, 1999.

We were permitted to invite our relatives to celebrate with us, Hank paid for my wedding gown, and we were married at the Barracks' Church of God in Christ in Baton Rouge, our capital city. The church was full of sisters and brothers, all praying for us and wishing us the best.

Both the wedding ceremony and reception went well. It was a beautiful day to be a bride, but the problem was that this bride was going home alone. We were legal in the eyes of God and the law, yet we were shackled by conditions and circumstances beyond our control. That night I cried myself to sleep. When I woke up during the night, I gave everything to God. Only He knew what the future held.

Needless to say, my family thought I had lost my mind—again.

It appeared that Hank was also ready to trust God's will for our lives. At least now, he talked about God. I felt that together we could make a difference in each other's life.

1 Peter 4:8

> *And above all things have fervent charity among yourselves: for charity shall cover the multitude of sins.*

It did not matter what others thought or the nature of the crime Hank had committed. I had my trust in God, knowing that He would never fail me. I was up in the clouds and did not want to come down. I felt as though I had married the President of the United States. Hank's incarceration meant nothing to me. I knew, in my heart that this, too, would pass. I trusted God to bless our marriage and now felt that I knew better what was required to make a marriage a success.

I even joked, telling Hank that I no longer cleaned baseboards. That had been one of his pet peeves. He said that he had been young and foolish, and that twenty-five years alone in prison had changed him.

In the Marines, everything had to be perfect, and that was how Hank had been with us. I told him that I would no longer live under the 1978 rules and regulations. I, too, had changed. And he agreed.

Psalm 34:8

> *O taste and see that the* LORD *is good:*
> *blessed is the man that trusteth in him.*

My sisters and brothers, God is good. He is a rewarder of those who continuously seek Him. He is good. I know, because He has been so good to me. I found the answer when I learned to pray to God and fellowship with Him.

Proverbs 3:5-6

> *Trust in the Lord with all thine heart;*
> *and lean not unto thine own understand-*
> *ing. In all thy ways acknowledge him,*
> *and he shall direct thy paths..*

I had begun to trust in a God who assured me that He would never fail me. I read in the Bible that He promised to direct my path, and I believed the words in the Bible were God's words.

Prayer and faith, I now knew, were the keys to unlocking doors, and I continuously encouraged Hank, telling him that Jesus would one day set him free.

Matthew 19:26

> *With men this is impossible; but with God all things are possible.*

Hebrews 11:6

> *he that cometh to God must believe that he is, and that he is a rewarder of them that diligently seek him.*

I kept preaching to Hank that Jesus was the answer and Jesus would set him free. I told him to look beyond his present circumstances.

2 Corinthians 4:18

> *While we look not at the things which are seen, but at the things which are not seen: for the things which are seen are temporal; but the things which are not seen are eternal.*

Circumstances were not in his favor, so we both had to realize that we were not in control; God was. A person can never accomplish their goal when their focus is on the present. Nevertheless, it was stressful trying to get him to focus totally on God and not the negative things of life.

Prayer and watchfulness was required to complete the task set before us. Fifty to life, statistically, was a shoeless, up-hill climb, but we were trusting a God who could do all things.

A Love Like Solomon's
(SOS 3:1-2)

In her bed at night,

with all her might,

she mentally sought the one she loved,

always thought of,

but could not find him,

her mood was dim.

She needed him.

She rose and went about the city,

through dangerous streets and hoods.

It was all for good.

She was seeking the one she loved.

the one she dreamed of,

her blessing from above.

But she did not find him.

He was hiding inside of her heart. [1]

Chapter 6

The Consequences of Our Decisions

2 Timothy 2:15

Study to shew thyself approved unto God,
a workman that needeth not to be ashamed,
rightly dividing the word of truth.

Behind every decision there is a consequence. Hank and could not afford to make any rash decisions. Many of life's choices are not orchestrated with God's purpose in mind, and the result is tragic. Therefore patience is vital. We had to be patient with God and offer Him no resistance. And the only way to be patient with Him was to trust Him. We continued to put our faith in God.

It's easy to write or speak those words, but the truth is: I chose to be with Hank even though things were not going as we had expected. The end result was on my agenda.

When I had agreed to visit Hank, I was under the impression it would be all smooth sailing. The parole board would see that his family had accepted him back, and he would be released and come home. He had used those very words to entice and convince me. The sad part about it is that I believed him. The reality of it was something altogether different. When Hank applied for parole, he was denied.

Psalm 46:10

Be still and know that I am God.

James 1:2-7

My brethren, count it all joy when ye fall into divers temptations; knowing this, that the trying of your faith worketh patience. But let patience have her perfect work, that ye may be perfect and entire, wanting nothing.

If any of you lack wisdom, let him ask of God, that giveth to all men liberally, and upbraideth not; and it shall be given him. But let him ask in faith, nothing wavering. For he that wavereth is like a wave of the sea driven with the wind and tossed. For let not that man think that he shall receive any thing of the Lord.

After two years of visiting Hank, my desire for him to come home began to overwhelm me. I needed wisdom to cope with the situation, much wisdom. Stressing out and crying would solve nothing. Only God could keep and guide me now.

A bulletin was issued that the prison would be transferring, with all of its inmates, to a new location. This meant that my commute would increase from an hour and fifteen minutes to two hours. I had to trust God.

Fear is of the enemy, and I needed to rid my heart of it. I could now attend church services, and I enjoyed them and felt myself getting closer to God. I begin to seek Him through this empty period of my life. He comforted me and our plight became easier to accept.

Now nothing else mattered but God. Hank had shackles on his hands and feet, but I, too, was shackled. My shackles were in my mind. The strange thing about all this was that I hadn't known that I was bound in this way.

Thank God for Jesus. It was Jesus Who loosed me from everything that had me bound.

1 John 4:18

> *There is no fear in love; but perfect love casteth out fear: because fear hath torment. He that feareth is not made perfect in love.*

The scheduled move occurred, visits and phone calls were placed on hold for about a month, and those few weeks were like months to me. Prayer was my only consolation.

Then, after a month, families were allowed to resume their visits, but the time permitted for each visit was now reduced from seven hours to three and a half. I didn't like that, but a little something was better than nothing at all.

Some may be thinking, "Why was this change so difficult?" Commuting back and forth (now four hours total) just for a three-and-a-half-hour visit was no joke. We had to plan precise arrivals, and I was up all night the night before preparing the foods I wanted to take. And all of this was now for just three and a half hours of time together. With God's help, I would do it.

Chapter 7

The Seeds of a Ministry

Jeremiah 33:3

Call unto me, and I will answer thee, and show thee great and mighty things, which thou knowest not.

Because of my situation, I began to seek ways to encourage other families and their inmates. When there is no Jesus, there is no stability. I wanted to become a counselor, to help the women of inmates in prison. I began to seek God for the wisdom to counsel those ladies. As I waited for Him to answer me, my walk with Him became closer, and I was now full of Jesus and wanted to do His work.

Hank noticed the change in me and said, for the first time, that he was able to see the light at the end of the tunnel. What that meant I wasn't sure, so I just answered, "Hallelujah!" I was just trusting the Lord for our future.

I pursued the Lord for His wisdom in counseling the ladies, and God can do anything. As I concentrated more on the needs of others, my burdens somehow became lighter, and I found the answers in deep and sincere prayers.

Once I learned to pray, I didn't give God a break. He gave me not only the confidence to overcome, but also the desire and strength to help others in the same situation.

I am a strong believer that there is no telling what God can do if we put my trust in Him. In the most difficult hour, when temptation occurred, Hank and I learned to lean on and depend on God.

Jeremiah 33:3

Call unto me, and I will answer thee, and show thee great and mighty things, which thou knowest not.

So, seek the Lord with all your heart and lean not to your own understanding. Seek God before making any decision, and learn to have confidence in Him to open doors.

He has told us to call on Him. Have you called upon Him lately? Spend some quality time with Him. Learn His voice and listen when He speaks.

The psalmist wrote:

Psalm 23:4

Yea, though I walk through the valley of the shadow of death, I will fear no evil: for thou art with me; thy rod and thy staff they comfort me.

God has promised:

Hebrew 13:5

I will never leave thee, nor forsake thee.

All those years I had refused to communicate with Hank I attributed to the fact that I hadn't yet forgiven him. Once I repented and forgave him, love was rewarded with love. Only God can do that.

Through obedience, I learned to trust in God. You can never work for God unless you sell out. Everything that wasn't of God had to leave my life. Playing games with God leads only to destruction. As I turned my life over to God, a change came over me. I learned that God was a

Keeper, and He will keep whatever you commit unto Him.

Now I went on a rampage, spreading the Word of God. I was called "crazy," because I continuously preached to the ladies, telling them to trust God to deliver their mates from prison. I suppose some of them must have said, "Well, her husband is in prison. What is she talking about?" But I had put all my faith and trust in the Lord, and I knew that He would eventually free Hank.

To speak and testify of the things I had learned about God brought me pure joy. There is no limit to what one can do through Christ Jesus. With Jesus as the center of your daily life, God will lighten your step. You will become a new creature. People will notice your new walk and your new talk. PRAISE GOD!

Hank, who knew me best, saw a change in me, and that delighted and challenged him.

Chapter 8

Working Toward Hank's Freedom

James 3:17-18

> *But the wisdom that is from above is first pure, then peaceable, gentle, and easy to be intreated, full of mercy and good fruits, without partiality, and without hypocrisy. And the fruit of righteousness is sown in peace of them that make peace.*

Let me stop right here. I need to clarify something. Although God blessed Hank many times, this book is not about what God did for Hank. It's about what He did for *me*. Accepting Hank into my life again was a plus. It led me to a closer walk with God. I knew that Hank and I both wanted his freedom, but it would take the will of God to bring it to pass.

When wanting God to intercede on your behalf, it takes wisdom, knowledge and understanding of the will of God. For without Him you can do nothing.

It takes Jesus Christ to mold and shape someone. You must be willing to accept the things you cannot change and be grateful for the ability to change, for the better, the things that you can. Seek and discover the will of God for your life.

In any relationship, dependency on Christ is mandatory. Not having Jesus equals chaos.

God spoke to Jeremiah:

Jeremiah 18:6

O house of Israel, cannot I do with you as this potter? saith the Lord. Behold, as the clay is in the potter's hand, so are ye in mine hand, O house of Israel.

Paul wrote to the Roman believers:

Romans 4:17

(As it is written, I have made thee a father of many nations,) before him whom he believed, even God, who quickeneth the dead, and calleth those things which be not as though they were.

Statistically, Louisiana's judicial and penal systems are among the toughest in the country, when it comes to releasing inmates. My family thought I was losing my mind. But what else was to be expected? A natural-minded man cannot understand the things of God. Oh, but I know that all things can be done through Christ that strengths us.

Hank had been given fifty years to life, but he learned to lean and trust on God. HALLELU-JAH!

It's easy to become distracted from your goals. Again, Paul wrote:

Romans 8:18

> *For I reckon that the sufferings of this present time are not worthy to be compared with the glory which shall be revealed in us.*

Philippians 3:13

> *Brethren, I count not myself to have apprehended: but this one thing I do, forgetting those things which are behind, and reaching forth unto those things which are before, I press toward the mark for the prize of the high calling of God in Christ Jesus.*

The enemy is always busy, and inflicting pain is one of his tactics. Trials and tribulations are inevitable. The Scriptures do not say that trouble will not come or will not last. But God's words, in the Bible, tell us how to defeat these little giants. It's through JESUS!

Through Christ Jesus we can overcome anything. We must pray, in season and out of season, knowing that God is on our side. Pray the Word and say the Word. Know, without a doubt, that whatever you ask, in the name of Jesus, it shall be done. Have faith and patience.

Then, we must ask in faith, believing God:

Isaiah 26:3

> *Thou wilt keep him in perfect peace, whose mind is stayed on thee: because he trusteth in thee.*

As noted in an earlier chapter, when I told Hank that I was free in Jesus Christ, he responded, "I now see the light at the end of the tunnel." I never knew what he meant by that, but I said, "HALLELUJAH, just the same.

Where the Spirit of God is, you are free indeed. Even behind bars, an inmate, through Jesus, can still be free. Hank thought I was as foolish as Job's wife when I told him I wanted him to speak freedom to the gates that kept him bound. For a time, that was his daily assignment.

But Hank began asking God to remove his shackles and to open the gates. I knew he did not understand that God could do anything but fail. I stood in proxy, on his behalf, at gatherings of believers in prayer, believing that God would set him free.

Jesus said:

Matthew 7:7

Ask, and it shall be given you; seek, and ye shall find; knock, and it shall be opened unto you.

We were back together, and that was all that mattered. All we had been through could never be explained, at least, not logically and understandably. But I was content.

All I can say is: through Christ Jesus, we can do all things. I learned to trust God to do the impossible.

Had I not faced some trails, there would not have been such a need for Jesus. Thank God for trials. Knowing that God would be there in the end, I learned to be bold in my faith.

I once wrote a message, "I Can See Clearly Now; The Rain Has Fallen." Rain falls in each of our lives. Oh, my sisters and brothers, despise not the rain in your life.

Romans 8:28

And we know that all things work together for good to them that love God, to them who are the called according to his purpose.

Oh, things will get better. Remember the rose. Look into your heart's eye, behold the rose, as it blooms. You are that rose.

In our lives, once the Word is planted and nurtured, we're able to come forth into the radiant light of Jesus Christ.

Chapter 9

Freedom At Last

Mark 10:9

What therefore God has joined together, let not man put asunder.

Just as we had believed and declared for so long, freedom finally came for Hank and he was granted parole. For some unknown reason, however, freedom was difficult for him. Readjusting to life outside proved to be his master. I really don't know why, but it was. His military ways were still there, but there was also something else I hadn't seen before. I couldn't explain it then, and I can't explain it now.

I had made plans for Hank's first day of freedom. I bought him new clothes and made plans to take him to dinner, but, as it turned out, he suddenly didn't have an appetite. Instead, he wanted to go visit his mother. I thought his first night would be *with me*. Oh, well, now we were on the highway to visit his family.

I was a little hurt. I had wanted to spend some quality time with my husband. But suddenly, all the plans we had made for his homecoming vanished. Through it all, I continued to be tolerant. For as long as I was able, I was patient with Hank, but eventually, it became obvious that his love for his family was far greater than his love for me. In time, we stopped communicating again, and he made me feel like I was his worst enemy.

All those years, walking through rain, sleet and storms to visit him and take him things, and now he didn't want me? In no time, his love for his wife had mysteriously waxed cold. Who could have imagined it?

I began to ask God where I had gone wrong. I began to cry out to Him, and He comforted me. It wasn't time for a rainbow. God was preparing me for something else.

For his part, Hank left me helpless, leaving me to go live with his mother, all because she told him she was lonely. At first, we would see each other only on weekends. I became his weekend bed-partner, and that was not what I wanted.

I wanted my husband at home in bed with me. I finally came to the decision that I would no longer play house on a weekend basis. Hank, didn't have a need to be home with his wife. He was focused on spending time with his relatives.

He knew better:

Matthew 19:5

> *For this cause shall a man leave father and mother, and shall cleave to his wife: and they twain shall be one flesh.*

Hank Miller had forgotten his promises to God.

Chapter 10

What Freedom Really Meant

Hebrews 10:33

Partly, whilst ye were made a gazing stock both by reproaches and afflictions; and partly, whilst ye became companions of them that were so used.

What did this all mean? Was Hank just using me to gain access to parole from prison? Had he intended to do the right thing and then was not able to live it out once he was free? It was all a mystery to me. What I did know was that the honeymoon was over (again). For some unknown reason, I still loved my husband, but he was gone from my life again.

I so dreaded the thought of my family, friends, and sisters and brothers in Christ knowing that my husband had deserted me. For ten years, I had traveled the highways every weekend, just to make him smile. Now that I was no longer needed, he cast me aside like so much garbage. It was devastating.

I decided that I would not allow my circumstances to put the Gospel to shame. I would accept the embarrassment of it all. And, at whatever cost, I would continued to be a wife to Hank, a faithful one.

Like the writer of Hebrews, I, too, was made a gazing stock, mainly by people who knew us. In whispers, they talked about the way Hank had treated me. Everyone who knew how I had stood beside him for so long and so faithfully were now scratching their heads. What could have happened?

The answer is that the enemy had blinded Hank Miller. That's exactly what happened. He began to feel that the grass was greener on the other side of the fence. It had happened before, and now it was happening again.

I was determined that this truly terrible turn of events would not rob me of my victory in Christ. His Word declares:

1 John 5:4

> *For whatsoever is born of God overcometh the world: and this is the victory that overcometh the world, even out of faith.*

To overcome the world is to gain victory over sin, and to become obedient to the Word of God. As long as you keep your eyes on the prize, which is Jesus Christ, you can be obedient.

When you've done your very best, The Lord Jesus Christ will remember :

Isaiah 41:10-13

> *Fear thou not; for I am with thee: be not dismayed; for I am thy God: I will strengthen thee; yea, I will help thee; yea, I will uphold thee with the right hand of my righteousness. Behold, all they that were incensed against thee shall be ashamed and confounded: they shall be as nothing; and they that strive with thee shall perish. Thou shalt seek them, and shalt not find them, even them that contended with thee: they that war against thee shall be as nothing, and as a thing of nought. For I the Lord thy God will hold thy right hand, saying unto thee, Fear not; I will help thee.*

James 1:3-4

> *Knowing this, that the trying of your faith worketh patience. But let patience have her*

*perfect work, that ye may be perfect and
entire, wanting nothing.*

When we fall, we *can* get up. God allows us to
choose right or wrong, and we live our lives of
joys and pains, choosing, but rarely spiritually.
It had taken me a while to believe there was a
God who knew me better than I knew myself, a
God who knew my every thought. If you don't
believe that, you don't know God. When I discovered just how awesome God was, it was a
scary moment. I was contemplating waving the
white flag and surrendering myself to Jesus, and
that's just what I did. I have no regrets for doing
that, and I never will regret it. How could I. Jesus
has given me a new life

Chapter 11

Hank Miller's End

Revelation 3:20

Behold, I stand at the door, and knock: if any man hear my voice, and open the door, I will come in to him, and will sup with him, and he with me.

Just two years after his release from prison, Henry "Hank" Miller suddenly died of a heart attack. He was just in his sixties, a relatively young man. Before he died, I fully believe that God allowed him to know that I loved him. God has said, *"Whosoever will, let him come."*

Was Hank ready to go? I really can't describe Hank's relationship with God. He talked enough about God and his faith in God that he was ordained while in prison. He was actually Rev. Henry Miller. He never interfered with my relationship with God. He had seen an improvement in my life, and he respected God and what He had done in me.

Was that enough? I can't say. Only God is the Judge. I know that Hank was grateful for the change in me, but I don't think he really understood that my loving him behind bars was the thing that had run me straight into the waiting arms of Jesus. He had sometimes said, "I'm not messing with Hilda and her God. She thinks she's the only one with a god." Again, God is the Judge. Each and every one of us needs to know God for ourselves.

I wouldn't want to leave you thinking that my marriage to Hank was entirely bad. When he was released from prison, besides his moods and military habits, he brought with him an occasional willingness to acknowledge God. That alone gave me hope. The best thing about our relationship was that I had found Jesus. Glory to God! So whatever I'd had to go through was worth it.

Chapter 12

My Beginning

2 Corinthians 5:18

*And all things are of God, who hath recon-
ciled us to himself by Jesus Christ, and hath
given to us the ministry of reconciliation.*

Another thing I received during my relationship with Hank was compassion toward
inmates. God wants us to love all men. We must
learn to look beyond a man or woman's faults
and see their need.

I was a new person in Christ, and I stood on
that. People began making remarks, "You're too
heavenly minded to be of any worldly good."
That was mainly because I didn't have a mate
and was not seeking one. "Life in this world
is over for you," some said. But they were so
wrong. My life had just begun.

Four and a half years passed. I lived those
years like Gideon at the wine press, hiding

from the Midianites. I hid from life, and from my occasional hurt and pain. But I learned, in whatsoever state I found myself in, to be content. After Hank died, I continued serving a God whom had yet to fail or forsake me. Glory be to His name!

Too many times, searching for love, I had failed God, but He has never let me down. In Jesus, I found true love. A never-ending love with Jesus, that's what I had found. As of this day, since accepting Jesus, He has watched over my every step. I chose to obey Jesus, and not man.

If you set your mind on the Author and Finisher of life, there can only be victory. Would I do it again? Yes. I was on a mission, and I found exactly what I needed in my life. I am more than grateful God counted me worthy to suffer and be led to Him.

Looking back to 1999 and al that followed, I say with the psalmist, *"If it had not been the Lord who was on our side,"* (Psalm 124:1) where would I be?" Jesus kept me and allowed me to become the woman I am today. He used a simple need for love to lure me into my husband's arms.

Because of Jesus, I became humble and caring, concerned for His people. I learned to look beyond the circumstances of the incarcerated and see only hope through Jesus Christ. My daily trials with Hank were only temporary. In the mist of it all, God began molding and shaping me into His image for the future.

If I had a chance to speak to Hank, I would say, "Baby, I forgive you. And I thank you for allowing the Lord to use you to draw me into His arms."

Before Hank, I'd had no real desire to serve God. I just wanted to live a normal life. But through reuniting with Hank and, thus, finding Jesus, I stopped everything that wasn't pleasing in the eyes of God. To keep this love I'd found in Jesus, I had to be faithful. Little did I know it, but God was calling me to be faithful unto Him for a purpose.

Now, this ends the first book, one story, but now another books begins. It is called *Suddenly* because it happened so suddenly. And, finally, you'll get your chance to meet Parenthesis.

(Yes, yes, yes!)

Book 2

Suddenly

Introduction

(Allow me to clarify this now. I am Parenthesis, Frederick (aka Ricky, aka Fred R. Ricks) Jones. I'm Rev. Lady's husband. Why am I called Parenthesis? There lies my domain. These two little quarter moons ( ) are parentheses, and I am confined to only speaking between them. They are my borders.

If it sounds like I'm complaining, I'm not. I'm thrilled to be a part of my wife's book. I guess you could consider me your chaperone for this story. I don't know if a story has ever been told this way before. Rev. Lady and I may be the first.)

Hilda: When are you going to get into the story?

(Girl, I mean, Darling, we have an audience. I was only speaking to them. I'll let you start the story.)

Chapter 1

What Suddenly Meant

Four and a half years after Hank died, I was lost in Faith, Hope and Love, the prison ministry that Hank and I had founded. Although loneliness had already begun to nibble at my heart, I knew that God wouldn't allow it to destroy me. He gave me strength and a purpose to be able to move on in life.

By then, both of my parents were deceased, and the endeavors of blending with my children and grandchildren were mainly lumpy, to say the least. I was sixty-four years old, an evangelist, and God, my twin granddaughters — Ja'Maya and Ja'Naya — and Faith Hope and Love Ministry, in that order, was all I wanted and needed in life. Ninety percent of my existence was centered around those three things.

Then, one summer evening, as I was tending my roses in the sweltering humidity of New Orleans, I noticed one particular rose laboring stubbornly to survive the suffocating heat. Then

I was pulled out of my comfort zone when a friend called telling me about a man who'd been in Angola Prison for thirty-eight years. Smiling, I returned to my roses. Little did I know: those roses were also special to someone who would become even more special in my life in the days ahead.

Within a few days, seemingly overnight, an infant rose appeared in my garden. And, like that rose, this new man suddenly appeared.

(Okay, that's me. Oh-oh, we'll talk later.)

As I was saying before I was interrupted, just as a rose suddenly appeared in my garden, this man also appeared, comforting me with words of feelings and wisdom, touching my heart in ways it had never been touched before. In his very first letter, he encouraged me. How did he know that, at that very moment in my life, I needed that specific encouragement? It had to be Jesus!

(People who encourage others also need encouragement. C'mon, Rev. Lady, don't look at me that way. I'm just letting people know why I said that. When can I say something?

Don't do this. Am I not your better half? Okay, okay, I'll let you get back to the story.)

Ricky's wisdom and honesty intrigued me. This very different man defied bars and miles to befriend me. As his friend, I became inexplicably attached. As noted, his first letter, without him being aware of the timing of it, encouraged me just when I needed encouraging.

I questioned the friend who called me concerning him, about his nature. She didn't know much. She told me he had a "flip mouth," meaning that he was outspoken. One of his favorite sayings was, "God don't raise cowards."

As I noted, since Hank's death, I'd been completely absorbed in God, my twin granddaughters, my ministry, and now out of the blue, here came this man, Ricky, a man who had been in prison for thirty-eight years for armed robbery, and he suddenly walked into my life.

Ricky's nature was sugary and solemn, and his simple passion for life was laced with his own romantic philosophies. He openly discussed his fears. He also spoke of a relationship with a pen pal, a married woman in another state, saying that she was the closest person to him.

(Rev. Lady, we were destined to become friends and then fall in love. All your past journeys pointed you in my direction. And, if I were in prison for only thirty-seven years, we wouldn't be together. It had to be thirty-eight years and twenty-one days, the day of our first encounter.

From the very beginning, as friends, we both felt an unexplainable connection. We were destined … . OK, back to the story.)

Just as he told me about his pen pal, he told her about me, and without warning, she ended their relationship. He didn't portray a macho image. He was hurt and didn't try to hide it. I was the only person he had to talk to, so he confided in me. I became his shoulder to cry on.

He couldn't imagine how grateful I was. If he did, he probably wouldn't have allowed me to comfort him.

(You're right.)

While consoling him, I explained to him that he was having a relationship with a married woman who was cheating on her husband. I asked, "What would stop her from cheating on you?" He wrestled with that for a couple of weeks, licked his wounds and confided more.

His letters became intense, yet he never flirted. He was always a perfect gentleman.

Within the pages of his letters, he began to show me a deeper side of himself. In an innocent way, I began to feel him out. As a friend, he became a part of me. He continued to pour out his soul on paper, and my heart absorbed it.

We confided in each other, secrets never before shared, and, in the process, something was awakening inside of me. This man's mind was so strong and filled with beautiful thoughts, concepts and creativity. He became my morning cup of coffee and cream. The man was real.

(I still am.)

Look, Rev. Lady's no fool. Ricky was real, and each day he moved up a notch higher on the reality meter in my estimation.

As a friend, he was a plus. This man, even though the was in prison himself, began to strengthen me. He had a concept and understanding on life that was only lacking Jesus. He harbored no hate or deceit. I had finally met a man with a clean and gentle spirit. God blessed me with Ricky's friendship, and I tried with all my heart to return the blessing.

(Look, writing a book with my wife isn't easy. She's very particular about things. Me, I'm more of an explorer.)

I am Rev. Lady, and I am sane. Because of Jesus, I have a forgiving heart, but, by no means, am I gullible. This man was no con-artist.

(No, not my style.)

He helped me through some stressful situations. He even let me know when I was out of the Spirit too long. He was a survivor. He had to be. He was there in that prison for thirty-eight years before our first encounter. Yes, there was a hardness in him, but it was a hardness mixed with kindness, wisdom, creativity and a very deep perception of things that cascaded from his core.

(Yes!)

Ricky became my ministry's Executive Director while he was still in prison. He was a writer.

(You're scanning my work now.)

He was also a poet, composer and vocalist. He worked with me on everything.

I desperately wanted to meet the man in person, so I applied for permission for a special visit, and my application was approved. The twins and I drove together to Angola. I was excited, plain and simple.

Oh, Lord, when I was first saw the man, I thought he was ugly, but when we sat at our table, his appearance seemed to have changed. That had to be God. Now his appearance complimented his attributes.

(Sounds like I'm laying it down a little thick, huh. Well, I'm not. I just described myself. Really, right now I don't want to take up too much time or, in this case, lines, but you should know by now that I am Parenthesis. Up to this point, we have been roaming the lines together. Further down the lines, I will share my thoughts with you. I guess I'll con-

tinue to flow between the lines. Someone's probably saying, "This book is a trip." Fact is, it's different.
Well, I'm outta here.)

And I'm back. He does that a lot, jumps on a page. I guess we'll get used to it.

(Parenthesis is not allowed to speak? I have thoughts and words, dreams and aspirations. Wait, before anyone gets the wrong impression, I love Rev. Lady. I am madly in love with her. She's my soul-mate. She's my everything.)

Flattery will get you nowhere. Now, back to the story.

Chapter 2

Friendship Turns to Love

In time, the friendship between Ricky and me turned to love, and I had never been happier in my life.

(I tell you now, my Love, I will love you with my last breath.)

I love you too, but we need to get back to the story.

Who would have thought that at sixty-four I would be given another chance at love? Suddenly, Ricky became a high percentage object of that chance. I was in the infant stages of something I wanted to preserve for as long as possible. Forever would be grandeur.

You see, I had never really known what real love was. I thought I knew, but I discovered that my past relationships had been only some form of infatuation.

What's wrong?

(I just deleted twenty-five pages. I clumsily deleted twenty-five pages, trying to write and type at the same time. Rev. Lady taught me how to basically use a laptop, and when I don't apply my full attention when using it, my hands are always hitting the wrong keys. Don't worry. If I didn't reveal my mistake, no one, upon completion of this book would have ever known. As I've said, we're on a joint venture in this book, and we believe that you, the readers, will experience sheer delight. We're all in this together.
Reverend Lady, you look worried.)

I'm not worried. It's just writing — your strong suit.

(It's just that I must recapture those feelings, knowing that one moment alters an emotion. It makes me think of the old saying, "Time heals all pain." But here's the difference: One moment you're happy to see an old friend, and the next moment their departure saddens you. It's too small to give much thought

to, but I apply that philosophy to all unpleas-
antness. I anticipate laughter whenever I cry.
It minimizes my tears.
By the way, I cry easily. I always wanted to
cry, but I kept a foolish image instead. I had
to survive. Oh, but now, whenever my heart
is touched, I weep.)

I guess you're wondering what happened in
this story. This is the present, and Ricky and I are
sharing ourselves with you, the readers. Ricky
came up with this concept of writing *Suddenly*.
I didn't understand it in the beginning, but I
trusted his mind.

(Excuse me, I know I'm not perfect, with my
often-grouchy ways and uncanny concepts,
yet I consider myself worthy of your trust,
for I have always been beside you since our
wedding night. And I will be beside you always. Thanks for your trust.
Since January 9th, 2015, we have never spent
a night apart. Being real, we're rarely apart
at any time. We live as one and are one with
God. I'm so glad you're my wife.)

I almost wasn't. May I reminisce? The night before our wedding, I began to have second thoughts. I was up at 2 in the morning. This was during the period when I thought Ricky had insomnia. As I was going to the kitchen, he spotted me and said, "I know you're unsure. Just don't be afraid. You are my destiny. You are my blessing from God, and it will be my duty to be yours for the rest of my life. By God's design, we were destined."

(Yes, we were. You influenced me to pray and within six weeks I told you I'd be free for Christmas. I put my trust in a God I had found in prison but had never prayed to until then. I know you thought I was crazy when I promised Ja'Naya and Ja'Maya I'd be home for Christmas. You asked me not to do that. You said you didn't want them [or me] to be hurt. I didn't want to hear any of that. But I continued. Now, I have two more promises to keep—Disneyland and this book.

When I promised the children I'd be home, I knew in my heart that I was going to be free. I told three people in prison during the Christmas season of 2014 that I would be free for Christmas 2015. They thought I had lost my mind. I knew one thing: God had forgiven me. My slate was clean. I hadn't prayed for myself in my life. I made a vow to God to do whatever I can to make life better for Reverend Lady.

And you always do. It's one of the reasons I love you so much. Each day, all through the day, I thank God for you.

(It's time.)

I still have a few minutes.

(You asked me to remind you. It's time for her to prepare. Now, it'll be just me and the reading audience.)

I'll be back in a few.

(There is so much I want to say. I guess I'll start here. You've probably already thought, not in a bad sense, about my serving forty years in prison. I was guilty of armed robbery and received a 198-year sentence. I prayed one prayer and said to God that if I ever went free it would be because of Him. From then on, I never prayed for freedom for over thirty-eight years. It was then that God blessed me with Rev. Lady.

Not barring the appeal process, I accepted my fate. I had made my bed hard and would lie on it. But I didn't give up. I made up my mind to live as long as I could and wanted to long as I lived. I knew that if I lived violently, I would die violently.

There were many dangerous men in prison, and I knew that in order to survive I had to think clearly. I began to reason and deduce everything. I got good at it. I worked on myself, reading many books until I wanted to write one myself. And I did.

I found that simplicity was beautiful. I began to see beauty in things most people overlook. My mind matured.

I say, "Man is mind, but woman is mind and matter; she reproduces." If a guy feels cheated, he should try giving birth.

I began to seek out beauty in everything. With reasoning, I was able to find a simple kind of peace. My outward appearance and antics were very deceptive. Humility had captured my heart.

I came to discover that prisons don't change people. A prisoner must want to change. Prison hardens many of inmates. No dungeons, terrible food, overpowering loneliness or field work can change a prisoner. A person must want it in their heart.

I should hate the thought of prisons, but I don't. In the beginning, the concept of prison had good intentions, but somewhere along the line, it became industrial and those intentions were lost in the dollars and cents of mammoth budgets. Prisons are now booming businesses. Rehabilitation is not even secondary. Those who change want to change.

Rev. Lady is frying fish. I hope I'm not boring you. I'm trying to paint a picture of myself in thought and concept. I can do that because prison poetry reveals my heart. C'mon!

As you read my prison poetry, keep in mind that I had not accepted the Lord yet as my personal Savior, and my language is sometimes crude. Please overlook it.)

Poems and Additional Commentary

by

Frederick "Ricky" Jones

You, Jesus

You are a sacred hymn,
lyrics awesome and divine.
In perfect meters to my heartbeat,
we dance like David into time.
You are the sun afire,
beaming my darkest gloom,
a streaking pastel rainbow,
the earth, the stars, the moon.
You are, indeed, the reason
for my heartfelt laughter.
You are the past, present,
tomorrow and day after.
You are my placidness
when I am girded by rage.
In the book of life,
You are on every page.
You are a sip of nectar
when bitterness consumes.
You are a miracle
when all seems doomed.
You are more than I deserve,
my every dream come true.
And I am truly grateful
to be dearly loved by You. [2]

Second Line Requiem

Tirelessly wading raging tides,
alight throughout the dash betwixt,
till dark waves rise,
consuming spirits' flight or plunge into Styx.
When lids fold to forever sleep,
memories, thus, are enshrined.
Recited eulogies abound,
then, a celebration of a Second Line.
A slow progression marches
mute to a groaning homage from brass.
Its lazy growl claims the still
of a life come to pass.
With solemn, revered calmness,
mourners fill cobblestone streets in perfect file,
marching slow, an umbrella'd, synchronized creep.
A trumpet's sudden wail
transforms the calm into frenzy,
the jazzy sound of Dixieland
through the ranks of many.
Dat Quartas then clinks lively,
bodies buck jumpin' around,
raising high those lowly spirits
for them bones goin' in the ground. [3]

Rise

Descending, tumbling over and over.

coulda, woulda, shouldas, parading non-stop

on dim mental corners,

where heart-troubling realities

offer mental lanterns no light.

Poised down low upon bended knees,

feeling like you can't get up?

Stop the pity party.

RISE!

Falling's only blemish is staying down.

A saint was once a sinner who fell and got up.[4]

(I hope someone's feeling me.)

Paradise

A tropical island of white-sand beaches,

towering palm trees

and gentle ocean breezes

comfort me inwardly,

helping to ossify this once frail thread of life,

braiding healthy strands

into an unbreakable rope.

Because of Jesus, I, unbroken, savor Paradise,

each simple breath inhaled. [5]

(I survived decades in prison, smiling inwardly, because I'd learned to find beauty in bad situations. The beauty of your worst nightmare is waking up from the dream. I marvel at simplicity, at simple things. Coming from a different perspective, I enjoy applying my, uh, uncanny, philosophical concepts. Please read on.)

The Sun and I

Blessings comfort these gnarled,

aching fingers, extending to claim freedom,

but grasping fistfuls of air

and reasons to be grateful throughout

each lighted span.

Each day I smile just for dawn,

wincing the taste of lime,

waking, no faith in luck nor charm,

gratefully served by your shine.

Dancing days, shackles and chains,

to bitter music heard sweet,

tossing through each lonely night,

dreams of two-steppin' beneath.

You sip day skies, I gulp,

each breath, unquenched.

In currents, I thirst,

tirelessly wading rising tides,

begrudgingly treading the worst.

And, sprout no magic, black nor white,

to conjure spreading wings,

for roaming endless days and nights,

to flee from all fettered things.

Still each day I'm blessed to greet

your warm and radiant face,

my bitter pangs flowing sweet,

my raggedness worn as new lace.

Come the day, my lids to clay,

your face to shimmer no more,

hurled into darkness, far away,

I, beyond those realms unexplored.

Till then, each night I lie

prepared for an early rendezvous

with your fiery, majestic glare.

I wake not. Farewell to you. [6]

A Dying Rose

Once a bed of roses was quietly in bloom,
each timid petal, a fresh, love's tune.
Their scarlet beauty captured the naked eye,
adorned the garden, bestowed visual highs.
Today a solitary rose stands all alone,
others of its mallow are withered and gone.
Its once prickly thorns
have weakened and fallen,
scarlet petals turned brown.
Death's voice is callin'.
Grey clouds overhead threatened to burst,
thus, to moisten its dryness,
to quench its thirst.
Autumn has crept upon,
so ever calm and slow.
One by one, its petals fall to mingle
with earth below.
Death was so close,
its fragrance completely worn;
outlived the others, to die alone.
It came to pass the rose was no more,
yet, still remembered, poetically adored. [7]

Hilda: I have a ways to go. Do you want to eat in here?

(You all go on and eat. I'll get something later. Right now, I'm a little absorbed by my own reflections.

Without me accepting Jesus as my Savior, God nurtured me. In prison, my thoughts were different from others.

Now, I want to share a little humor.)

Socrates

Melancholy, thus, boredom's mark,
decided on a strolling walk,
visit the zoo in the park,
see what wonders lie.
Standing before a monkey, caged,
our orbs locked in a staring gage,
I, unaware of the inner sage
hidden within his eyes.
At that very moment of time,
to greet the chimp I was inclined,
But mischief folly filled my mind
These words, I spoke, deride;
"Hey, chimp, tell me your name," I mocked.
Then mocked again, "Talk to me now,
and claim your fame."
SUDDENLY, aware were his eyes.
"Well, I guess you've nothing to say,"
I teased before walking away.
But all at once, I felt dismay,
shocked by his shattered guise.

"Sir, please stay, I'll chat for a while,"
He SPOKE with an awkward smile,
adding, "My wisdom is a mountainous pile.
Tis' here true knowledge lies."
SUDDENLY, I was mentally inverted,
My acuity silently blurted,
"Spoke? This beast I'd flirted?"
This cannot be, thought I.
He said, "I presume you are shocked,
but I am more likely than a verbal rock,
and the very last of prating stock.
So please abandon your surprise.
As you wished, lets chat for a spell,
for I am truly bored as hell.
There is so much to tell
before the bell tones for our parting goodbyes.
You may address me as Socrates.
Would you please stop gawking at me,"
he sighed.
"Ah, the jungle trees,
from branch to branch I'd fly."
Dumbstruck, I mumbled, "You're talking."
He quipped, "Not harder than walking."

I stared. He said, "Or gawking,
or eagles learning to fly."
Right then, he scratched his head,
thoughtfully suspired as if burdened with lead,
and to me, these words he said:
"Of your kind, many things I despise
I despise your selfishness
and pitiless minds;
great intellect used for greed is your crime.
If only you'd stop to draw a line,
one not beyond the stars.
You forfeit peace in favor of wars,
waging them nigh and afar,
dreams of conquest of the stars.
Tell me, is this a lie?
You look shocked, taken aback.
It is a fact, cheating and lies is your act,
doing so, straight stares, eye to eye,
without compromise.
You claim to be an advocate of the Holy Word,
but the truth, to you, is unheard,
Your reasoning is absurd.
"Tell me, is this a lie?"

Lowly and slowly, I shook my head,
absorbed by what the chimp had said,
this simple beast, my mind he read,
said, "The truth gleams in your eyes.
But, harken, for I've more to say.
You defy God and tell others to pray.
Corruption and bigotry is your way,
yet justice is your cry.
My words, though harsh, speak the truth.
You've all but lost your flouting youth.
Your elder's bane seeds
have destroyed their roots,
assuring a callow demise.
Drugs, violence, envy and hate,
tyrant egos vying for greatness,
compassion's value has no weight.
Your well of love is dry."
"Socrates," I cried, please say no more.
Woe am I for opening this door!
Your silence I implore."
Then, there we held each's eye.
"This chat," he said, "has been rather nice,
but do believe, it shan't happen twice,
save two bananas, that is my price."
Then, there, our parting goodbyes. [8]

(For many, many years, I viewed the world from the inside out. I romantically said that I was in a bubble. From the inside, with much diplomacy, I'd scrutinized worldly problems.

Please hear me, governmental laws and amendments will not fix the problems of the world. The path to fixing it is simple, but because of evil—Satan, the devil—the simplicity of traveling the path is filled with deceit.

LOVE can fix anything, and Jesus is love. It's all in the Bible. We need to love more.

Is this book crazy or what? SUDDENLY! I am Suddenly. No, no, I am Parenthesis, book chaperone. Yeah, I'm smiling.

You're not disturbing. Say what you want to say.)

Hilda: I know you're enjoying Ricky's poetry. He sent thousands of handwritten pages home, but they were lost during Katrina. Well, it's time for me to eat and clean the kitchen.

(Allow me to take you on another poetic venture. In my mind I questioned everything.)

Questions

Does divine entwine delight

for true smiles every crease?

Perhaps, a bridged gap helps to perceive

an understanding out of reach?

Why faith comes and goes?

Maybe we're all deceived?

We fool ourselves to rule ourselves ...

Tis' not easy to believe?

Indiscrete, do fools secrete

when opening their mouths?

They rave and prate till [oops, too late],

secrets are spread about.

Did wise men think with a drink?

A sanguine brew from the urn,

then billed their fills as skills enhanced,

a trait that churns and burns.

Are the dead more than before,

or just a corpse in the grave?

Where do spirits go?

I just don't know,

but many a mouth do rave.

How far is the tiniest star,

a wee speck in the sky,

whose plight adorns twilight

in the twinkling of an eye?

Do prophets really predict?

Perhaps, it is a gift,

or maybe the fruit-bearing truth

is one's burden to lift?

Does a nightmare scar the heartless,

unable to feel?

Does hate reign for no gain,

but to mar love's appeal?

Through delusions and confusion,

are questions repeatedly mistaken,

possibly waiting for answers to awaken? [9]

(Want some more? I will take you a little deeper. I loved my mother, but I hurt her with my choices.)

Dust To Dust

Through hindsight, I see clearly,
the many heartaches caused
by my repeated failures,
those bedamn lapses that made your life
a barefooted walk on burning coals,
bearing burdens of forgiveness
with each weary and determined step.
Ashes To Ashes, Dust To Dust,
I pen this poem, thinking of you.
From Dust To Dust,
returned, then consumed by the earth
to be a part of an endless cycle.
And your memory filled with mirth,
eclipsing sadness in its wake,
storing tears in clouds until,
as raindrops,
they fall and mingle

with murky, watered memories
of my once-thrashed conscious.
And from afar, the wind sings, "Prisscillaa."
And from afar, your laughter,
a gentle pitch, I strain not to hear.
Through the dust lying on these rusted chains,
your nudging presence looms tenderly,
quickening the healing of my wounds,
but when it gathers beneath my lids,
tear drops, stingy trickles, fall
like lazy drops of dew
down an aging tree.
Thinking of you,
I weep with an unbroken smile,
dancing into the future without you. [10]

Dedicated to Priscilla Marie Jones

(1927-2001)

Love you, Momma

Embrace

In my life, I have stooped low enough
to crawl with snakes,
stepped on innocence,
exposed like chocolate under the sun,
leaving my prints in a chocolaty mess.
This memory, I embrace as I would,
saying good-bye to the woman too afraid
to return my love.
A less than enchanting story
of one man's transformation
from a bloodied, clinched fist,
to a gentle, scribing hand.
Grateful, I embrace the wedge
as I would a floating log,
while shipwrecked at sea.
Fully aware that I am to blame,
I tread this cesspool,
filled with life's runny waste,

from the churning bowels of this iron-crib.

This acceptance, I embrace

as I have His mercy.

Bending only to exercise my wrought-iron will,

forged by God, stands upright

in this grim place,

where wills broken like dried twigs.

Humbly, I embrace this trait

the way I wanted to my mother,

while she laid in her coffin.

What a blessing to revel

in thoughts of a divine place

where we are free from all pain.

I embrace this promise,

as I would His bloodstained feet,

for His gift of salvation.

My mind stays afloat

by building mental dams,

to contain the rising anguish

threatening to inundate hope.

As I sit on the banks of an unknown river,

I embrace this ability

as I wish I could have,

my father's hand.

The welcome dreams of roaming,

soaring high above snow-capped peaks,

free as a stirring breeze

beneath a bird's spreading wings.

I embrace these dreams

as I would my beloved,

kissing her over and over again.

I will dance long as I can

and want to long as I dance,

embracing the music,

both bitter and sweet,

till He wraps me for all eternity. [11]

Spring

Winter's demise is confirmation

of God's promise of animation.

Chirping birds are heard in their nest,

frolicking critters consume morning's sun,

the chill has been lain to rest.

Ah, to witness what has begun.

Colorful feats in process,

once nigh to earth, ascending more.

Simple wonders for all to digest,

umm, a scrumptious lore.

Bees on nectar sprees bestir.

It's their span to pollinate.

Tirelessly they whisk and whir

a rarely viewed display of greatness.

On dew-laced greenery, all claim their place,

each pose naturally declared,

each perfectly-painted face,

rich and alive, no longer bare.

Firmly, SPRING stakes her claim,

seducing many a heart.

Hallelujah! Praise God's name.

O, How Great Thou Art!

Come a time, spring disappears,

seems fleeting, this moving trend.

No need worry, no need to fear.

With grace, SPRING comes again. [12]

(In prison, I lived inside of my head. I had made the world [in my thoughts] a beautiful, poetic place of reason. I came to realize that ugliness was easy to find. Then, I began to reason: if finding ugliness was easy, finding beauty would be the same. All we need to do is look for it. There is beauty in waking up clothed in your right mind and healthy. If all you look for is ugliness in life, you become ugly—ugly on the inside. And that's where it counts with God.

Each day of life there is so much to be thankful for, and if you're grateful, it's because of finding some form of beauty in life. There is an unbelievably joyous beauty in being grateful. Measure yourself by how grateful you are.

Now, how about some more poetry? Okay, let's roll.)

Savior

Prophesied	Son
King	Lamb
Messiah	Tempted
Obedient	
Teacher	Amazing
Admonisher	Merciful
Just	Healer
Truth	Way
Light	Challenged
Despised	Accused
Persecuted	Betrayed
Surrendered	Judged
Convicted	Beaten
Ridiculed	Suffered
Crucified	Wept
Forsaken	Died
Resurrected	SAVIOR [13]

(Thirty-three words, one for each year of His life.)

(Here's what I think about marital commitment.)

One Vow

Paired with budding commitments,

each as bright as sunshine,

tenderly waring twain hearts.

But, when teardrops descend

upon the budding pact, like unforeseen rain

from suddenly-gloomy clouds,

there, in those hovering hordes,

one vow lies hidden,

lost beyond the thin line,

in a place where love's burning passions

are dimmed to weakened embers.

By the power of God,

Hearts are merged as ONE,

forever and always:

"Till death do you part." [14]

(My thoughts carried me through prison.
Please remember that.)

Whispers in the Wind

As the wind bobbed slowly,

enticing the twirling of leaves,

I heard an unfamiliar whisper

uttered through the breeze.

Through the gentle passing,

these few words were spoken,

"See My world around you,

though troubled, it is yet unbroken."

I'd been lacking in spirit,

never prayed, even to gain,

not even from weighty burdens

causing my heart to pain.

Hearing those words,

fueled an urge to pray.

I was filled with peace and hope.

All chafe had gone away.

Right then, I knew how blessed I was

to feel the breeze,

see the far horizon,

hear birds singing in the trees.

Dust devils swirled around me.

Fragments were spiraling in the air.

The sacred moment nudged

and stripped my lacking bear.

More, a gentle breeze,

orchestrates music for dancing leaves.

Through an unbroken calm,

I whispered, "Thanks,"

through each breeze. [15]

(My life became one day at a time. Tomorrow's only beauty is Heaven, and I hadn't accepted Jesus as my Savior yet. Still, it became easy for me to find beauty in a day. It was a task beyond that. Each morning, I got out of bed, wanting and trying to be worthy of the beauty I'd found in one day of life. More poetry? By the way, I am having a wonderful time.)

Dawn to Dawn

Early, before the morning sun,
when darkness is on the run,
there, mingling with the infant morn,
are sweet musings,
so tender, so warm.
And when my lids close come night,
there in darkness, my candlelight,
His proximity, my guiding beam,
from dawn to dawn,
reality and dreams.
Each day I wake, this life to mesh,
obliged for the day,
hoping the next would steer me forever nigh
to being the apple of Your eye.
And when I rest, forever in sleep,
let not a single mourner weep
my not waking to greet dawn,
for I will be wrapped in His loving arms. [16]

(From dawn to dawn is the span of a day. One day at a time ... , that was my key to finding peace. Then, suddenly, I met Reverend Lady, and now we're writing this book together. Ours is a somewhat romantic tale. God prepared us for one another. Now, we're together as husband and wife.

I'm always jumping around. I want to share something about problems. Don't let problems stress you out. When you think of problems, allow it to be in assessment of a solution. If you're not thinking of a solution, you're enhancing the problem. While you're stressing, the problem yet breathes. Also become aware that, in a very strange way, we need each other just to be. Allow me to explain: The sexiest woman in the world, by standards, is measured by the contrast between overweight and underweight women. Without them, her shine loses some of its luster. If it weren't for ugliness, beauty loses some of its appeal. It takes a skinny or fat man to enhance a muscular man's body.

Here are some more of my favorite quotes:

Beyond simple beauty is ugliness.
A good lie is the truth sprinkled with deceit.
Joy is measured by gratitude.

I now depart.)

Hilda: I'm back. I won't be doing much more tonight. I had a hectic day, and it will be worse tomorrow. Parenthesis, or whatever his name, is eating. So, good night.

(I am wordlessly extinguished and will wake up with a smile.)

Hilda: Suddenly, Ricky ...

(Please! Okay, okay!)

Hilda: Suddenly, Ricky walked into my life. Before I was able to see him, and with many miles between us, I was able to feel him so easily, through his letters. I know it was only mentally, but I immediately saw that his mind was extraordinary. I had never encountered thoughts and concepts even remotely close to his. His letters went from passing time to prime time in no time and left me trying to read his inner thoughts.

Even from prison, he helped me through a lot of things, and when I didn't listen to his logic, I wished I had. He has something to say.

(Greetings! We are here this day because of God's grace and mercy. I hope sleep was peaceful and dreams were pleasant. I was sharing some of my quotes. Here are a few more.)

Peace is impossible without love.

A billion dollars can't be compared to eternal life.

If evolution is true, what happened to the rest of the apes?

The ultimate love for mankind is Jesus.

Love is complicated, but hate is very simple.

War is ruler verses defiance, often with greed betwixt the two.

Disrespect and politics are the best of friends.

Most rich people are spiritually broke.

(My quotes are not meant to offend anyone. They come from my logic and reasoning, but, if I've offended anyone, forgive me. I apologize.

The one who doesn't feel the need to be forgiven has the heart of a potential murderer. The old saying, "Three things are for sure: taxes death and trouble," has always been wrong. What about Heaven and Hell? That makes five.

People worshipped Greek and Romans gods both before and after Jesus' death and sacrifice. Many didn't believe then. Can you imagine the tally of believers in 2018?

I'll return with some more quotes. I know my concept of writing this book has been strange, but if you've made it this far, I know I'm working with a little something-something. That's my street side making its presence felt—"a little something-something."

I have more poetry to share. Enjoy or, ah, delight yourselves. But before I share more poetry [I'm smiling now], I need to say this: Today I met a guy with a placard that said "John 3:16" on the back of his vehicle. I greeted him and was compelled to give him a testimony. I know, that our meeting was God's work.)

Man with a Gun

Unexpecting, wife and kids,
now memories on a shelf,
a sad family tragedy.
He even killed himself.
MAN WITH A GUN ...
Innocent bodies strewn in malls,
concerts and schools,
massacres without warning,
a game without rules.
MAN WITH A GUN ...
A speeding vehicle on a neighbor street
leaves carnage behind
for everyone to see.
MAN WITH A GUN ...
A crowded market
finds no one aware
of death's forthcoming,
Its stench in the air.
MAN WITH A GUN! [17]

Toasting War

WAR ...
compassion buried the weight
of unjust justification.
WAR ...
glory and righteousness distorted,
a wall of names of the many fallen,
violence spilled upon domestic soil,
crumbling majestic, towering twins.
WAR ...
in its fury, promotes killing
and dying for country
as an act of honor.
WAR ...
mimicked by children beneath blue,
spacious skies
of neighborhoods and city streets.
WAR ...
a quick remedy for ailing peace.
WAR ...
a bitter brew, repeatedly gulped,
and in drunken stupor.
Around the world,
brimmed glasses are held high,
spilling and staining Mother Earth's skirts. [18]

Overflowing
(Mentality for War)

During the Alpha span,

in the wake of Eden's breech,

it inhaled a deep breath

and exhaled a dense mist

of shameless vanity.

The flesh became alive!

Selfishness arose.

An OVERFLOWING

spread over the earth.

Religions, races and families

destroy one another.

Never spontaneous,

war and violence destroy

God's plan for harmony

before any blood is shed. [19]

Raining Tears
(The Sadness of War)

The rolling hordes, darkly dressed,
depict times we mourn
while God distributes rest,
gives comfort the storm.
Each torches' bright, streaking light,
veined the hordes ebon wings,
a dirge of this rumbling plight.
I can hear them singing: "It's raining tears"
from sources deep,
cascading upon the faithless sane.
It's raining tears,
everyone's weeping tears of sorrow and pain,
raining tears, often hidden,
too much for speed to drain.
It's raining tears when love's forbidden.
Tears fall just like rain.
It's raining tears from heartless decrees,
tears the system won't claim,
raining tears when it's hard to sleep,
nightmares, again and again.
It's raining tears, no shepherd, lost sheep,
tears fall just like rain.

It rains tears inside each cell.
Reasons can't be explained.
It's raining tears. Can anyone tell
tears are falling like rain?
It's raining tears, marching to war,
tears, pouring like a hard rain.
It's raining tears in shimmering drops,
tears for each senseless slaying.
Tears ... will they ever stop?
Tears keep falling like rain.
Too many tears, flooding wraths.
O, let them not be in vain,
for selfish tears make fire laugh.
Yes, tears are falling like rain.
It's raining tears full of yearning,
trickling again and again,
smiles upside-down, eyes burning.
Tears falling, falling like rain.
It's raining from joys so few,
smiles and laughter lame,
raining tears, not grasping the truth.
Only God can stop the rain. [20]

(My life in prison came down to a couple of options: (1) To find peace each day until I died or (2) To become a miracle. And, in between that, I had the task of making myself a better man each day. I became a miracle. It may be a very small miracle to some, but not to me. I HAD NO WAY OUT OF PRISON! O, yes! It was a miracle! I am not crazy, but I would have died in prison without tears. I just didn't want to be buried there. Right outside of the gates would have been okay, but I didn't want to be buried on those fordding prison grounds.

How about more poetic expressions?)

Forget Me Not

O, let not the thought of me
fade away or rot.
Don't let that be, I beg of thee.
My few friends, forget me not.
When my voice is silent,
my face not seen,
I will be inside the tunnels
of memories and dreams.
Please, store me within your heart,
secure the door, and keep it locked.
A thought away I will be.
My few friends, forget me not! [21]

21. Copyright © 2018 by Frederick Jones

I Ponder Dying Alone

I'm often pondering dying alone,

facing the unknown,

a chill in my bones.

What will become of me?

Would my eyes yet see?

Another ship lost at sea.

O, let God be near,

to ease my fears,

dry, if any, my tears.

If I, dressed in spiritual lace,

could only see His face,

thank Him for His mercy and grace.

I need to be strong, right all my wrongs,

before I move along.

Death has come, shall come again,

who knows when?

I can't predict the end.

All I know is: when I die,

I will be too big to cry.

The real deal of what I'll feel

when my coffin is sealed?

What lies in the ground?

Sounds something profound?

Hell or Heaven bound?

So many thoughts in my mind,

refined dirges in double time.

Most of my life, these thoughts unknown.

Now, I ponder DYING ALONE! [22]

Feast

Thrice a day, stomachs growling to be sated,

a file of eagerly-moving prisoners

visits the chow hall.

A seemingly jovial chatter fills

the cinder-block building,

as stiff, plastic spoons move

in swift upward motion,

from worn trays to mouths,

performing their chore.

Thoughts of Whoppers and fries.

Ain't none of that,

just chow, prepared not for taste,

but mere consumption.

Damn you, Hunger!

You make me wanna SCREAM.

Beans, beans, beans and more beans.

But I ain't starving.

I go to the chow hall,

get my vapid issue and eat it

with little chewing.

People don't starve in prison

(unless they want to).

We're fed three times a day.

It may not be yum, yum, really want some,

but we ain't starving like all those shabby,

barefooted children on hunger commercials,

with their huge sad eyes

and tormented smiles.

What we gripe about

they would consider a feast.

Damn you, Hunger!

You make me want to SCREAM!

Beans, beans, beans and more beans.

But I ain't starving. [23]

(I was never a victim of hunger, and my thoughts had grown wise enough to realize that my situation was nothing. There were many people less fortunate. I defeated my woes, being grateful for one day of life. I found myself at peace with the world. I lived one day at a time, with this attitude: whatever I encounter today, good or bad, is my cross to bear. Waking up, especially without God, guarantees no glee. Bitter or sweet, it's my treat. I'm rhyming and smiling.)

The Guard and I

From the light of dawns,

descending into nights, inside this tomb,

trimmed with razor wire

and manned guard towers,

you and I do our time,

watching one another closely,

not hating, but objectively,

you, as a means of income,

I, merely to survive.

Together, we make an inverse design

on the fabric used for tarp to cover the truth,

the whole truth, and nothing but the truth.

Often, I peep you watching me,

and I know you know,

I, too, am watching you.

I would trade places with you,

get away from all this madness,

even if, just for a half day,

spend some quality time with my family,

tell my kids exaggerated tales

about this wretched place,

hoping to scare and stir em' away

from all this madness,

so they wouldn't become

a pattern of inverse design

on the fabric used for a tarp

to cover the truth, the whole truth,

and nothing but the truth. [24]

Boneyard

Sinewy tendons wrapped around
the acing bones of withering men
clutching crusted-over doubt
and hope to defiantly thwart years,
like mountains beneath the sea
or old crumbling tombstones
in decaying graveyards,
where lost spirits, in limbo,
scream for mercy and forgiveness.
And, though often hard to feel,
God, watching from above,
is discretely called upon
to comfort the weary bones,
trying to conquer time.
I say, until the sure passing of sleep,
never to awake,
the sweet thoughts of roaming
help to bear the wretched fates
of antique grandfather clocks,
ticking toward a predetermined destiny
for prisoners, hard-laboring
through prolonged death sentences
executed by time. [25]

Dancin'

Regardless of the many years,
listening to bubbled tunes
and reminiscing paper dreams,
I'm two-steppin' the dash,
dancin' to the dirge
of couldas, wouldas and shouldas.
Once upon a time,
I, with two left feet,
tried to rule the dance floor.
Oh, but now, deep in the crevices
of dawdling day-by-day time,
I am dancin' to the rhythm of music
caressing me inwardly.
I'm like Michael,
a dancin' machine,
or M. C. Hammer's
Can't Touch That, Devil,
and even with the chances
of dancin' my last dance in this bubble,
I'm two-steppin' the dash
and will continue to,
as long as God plays the music. [26]

10,957 Days

For the past thirty years,
I have died over and over, so many times.
Befriending death seemed befitting,
but because of grace and mercy,
that ground, unbroken,
has been transformed into clay
and kneaded into passions,
parched with deep remorse,
a fresh earthenware,
saved, scorched memories.
10,957 DAYS of fish-walking this cesspool,
always mindful of roaming,
staying afloat only
because of His will's buoyancy.
For thirty years, 10,957 DAYS,
I have pained greatly,
at times, the pain so overwhelming,
my mind would fold
into a fetal position
and rock to tunes often waning
inside the shrieking chaos of this madness.
Yet, even then, His voice
pierced those dissonant sounds. [27]

Riding the Wave

It has never been easy,
staying atop hopes and dreams.
Through gloom-streaked days,
to rarely seen starry nights,
I tread doggedly,
yearning to roam afar,
or even nigh,
just beyond the guarded entrance
of this will-breaking surf,
who, without masticating,
devours time and surfers in chunks.
Wishing to be untangled
from webs spun yesterday,
but ain't no bottled lady granting three,
not even one.
I shouldn't have been fisted,
should have been straight, but I was twisted.
No balance at all.
Still, it's never easy riding the wave,
and if it seems it is,
it's only because of His grace and mercy.
I'm riding the wave,
for through Jesus,
I'm learning the art of balance,
and each day, I get better. [28]

Enemy L. D.

He is a nemesis unto himself,
constantly complaining,
cursing the present, future
and ghosts from a haunting past.
A fatherless childhood shades
his deep scars of abandonment
and siblings' rivalries aged.
He gobbles yummy memory
of a weird kind of love,
always craving more
to sate his ravenous appetite.
Twenty-five at fifty,
a dagger into his heart
for his fatal bullet into another's.
Bearing his loathed cross,
trudging it bitterly,
unable to go backward.

Begrudgingly moving forward,
halfheartedly fighting demons,
licking his wounds with little patience
for a loitering mending process.
Lungs filled with stale air expand,
reeking those nigh the stone
poised above his drooping shoulders.
He anoints himself as innocence,
victim by the cracks in life's surface.
White banner never raised,
in pity, he battles himself.
He is his own enemy. [29]

(By no means, am I a psychiatrist, but I do know that I had to use some type of psychology to be able to survive over two thirds of my life in prison. You see, to me, psychology is merely a form of reasoning. In our everyday lives, we need to apply more reasoning. As they say, "A mind is a terrible thing to waste." It's one of my favorite quotes.)

Easy

Everything was Easy,
easy like Sunday morning.
A sad loss was Easy.
Always yakking was Easy.
A boyish charm and humor was Easy.
A class act was Easy.
Humbleness was Easy.
Training to reclaim the belt was Easy.
The relentless shadow boxer,
with sharp combinations, was Easy.
Living simple was Easy.
Dying unexpectedly was Easy,
easy like Sunday morning
or a Friday afternoon.
Now, Easy is a memory,
sure to melt away with time.
Right now, it's hard. [30]

In memory of Felix "Easy" Green.
He died while training for his big fight.

Ode To W.H.

Within an inky slumber,

she reached,

touched me profoundly,

praising Bacca's ascent.

Awakened by her words,

I, too have been resurrected

from a word-torn grave,

burning with penning passions

never to extinguish. [31]

Captivity

So many stories to tell
about this living Hell
devouring empty shells
in CAPTIVITY.
Time seems to stop,
stars above seem to drop,
seems too low to reach the top
in CAPTIVITY.
Peace of mind barely exists,
remembering well the outer mist.
Only God offers bliss
in CAPTIVITY.
Lost within a smoky haze,
petty rules mentally raze,
making hard to trek the maze
in CAPTIVITY.
Before detains each after,
fear grows faster,
quelling all laughter
in CAPTIVITY.
A hunger in every bone,
kings and queens dethroned,
dreading being alone
in CAPTIVITY.

Remembering the bling
and other material things,
now Blues, the song we sing
IN CAPTIVITY.
No ally through thick and thin
who won't deceive or pretend
it's hard to find a friend
IN CAPTIVITY.
O, where is the key,
needed to set me free?
Only the dead flee
IN CAPTIVITY.
What's needed to compensate,
to lessen my burden's weight?
Hopelessness is so great
IN CAPTIVITY.
Hindsight came a little late.
To beam my darkened fate for freedom,
I wait and I wait
IN CAPTIVITY.
Lord, hear our cries and calls.
Be prompt, make haste, do not stall.
With Your Spirit, free us all
IN CAPTIVITY. [32]

Playground

Just imagine, a PLAYGROUND

deep in the hood,

with no drugs or violence,

one with far greater joys

than monkey-bars, sliding boards,

merry-go-rounds and swings.

A PLAYGROUND of fun and happiness,

filled with all the simple things

needed to make children smile,

especially, parents who support them

with love and kindness.

A PLAYGROUND blessed with God's presence

and never-ending vigilance.

A PLAYGROUND of dreams fulfilled,

where St. Nick visits throughout the year,

leaving gifts for everyone,

and Bill Cosby is President,

thus, pools of Jello abound.

A PLAYGROUND governed by children,

and adults are law-abiding.

No birthdays are ever forgotten.

All children are pet owners.

Parents are forbidden to argue,

fight, divorce, separate,

or be in drunken stupor.

Imagine a PLAYGROUND deep in the hood,

one where children enjoy childhood

and dream the dreams of a child. [33]

The Light

Within the spirit realms,

deep inside my abyss,

there was blinding darkness.

Afraid, I stumbled,

fell and lost my way.

I began searching frantically for light,

only to lose myself in the dark.

On my knees, bewildered,

I silently called out His name—JESUS!

Suddenly, there in the darkness,

my eyes beheld a tiny spark,

no more than a wee speck,

that gradually brightened.

I had found Jesus,

the Light of the World!

Indeed, where there is light,

there is hope. [34]

Color Me Black

Pondering the dark sheath
covering my anatomy,
I discovered a beauty too many neglect to see.
I now realize how my childhood influences
brimmed lasting apprehensions
toward the color black:
Darkness was frightening,
black cats were bad luck,
black clouds meant unsavory weather,
mourners dressed in black.
To the naked eye, black was foreboding,
but beyond those dogmatic perceptions
were hidden truths to treasure:
Genesis 2:7 states,
Man was formed "*of the dust on the ground.*"
I began to reason:
darkness without fear is tranquil.
A white cat is unlucky
(if that's what you believe).

Black sheep aren't outcasts;

they are unique.

Dark clouds bring forth rain.

The fluid of life is for those paying homage

to paupers and kings alike.

Darkness gives power to light.

Regardless of color,

seeking the worst in anything

comes with a guarantee to find.

The same applies when searching for good.

Looking hard is required,

but it will also be found.

Referring to people and color,

black and white are counter opposites,

blending in unbalanced patterns,

white being the dominant shade,

yet by perfect design,

unsung, dark silhouettes are throughout. [35]

Read On

When fooled by illusions

from mass confusion,

never cringe in the haze.

You'd be amazed,

if you'd just turn the page and READ ON.

When you're empty inside,

with little will to survive,

be daring and brave and never afraid

to turn the page and READ ON.

When it's hard to prevail,

for your heart's been derailed,

and your tears come in rolling waves,

don't ponder the grave.

Just turn the page and READ ON.

When the sun doesn't shine,

there's a light you must find

to rekindle the blaze

that brighten your days,

by turning the page

and READING ON.

When prating enemies

are nigh realities,

let them bellow and rave.

You're a star on HIS stage.

So just turn the page

and READ ON.

The Sacred Book of Life

speaks much toil and strife,

yet many are the green pastures

within every chapter,

but you must turn the page

of your Bible and READ ON. [36]

(My thoughts carried me through prison, and
now it's a blessing to share them with you.)

Burning Songs

Sugary verses of oft-ragged,

rhymed meters,

yet occasionally nebulous,

as double-standard laws.

Scribbled in the smoky muss

of penning obsession,

vague verses were submerged

in the waters where my

heart sips unquenched

and aspirations dog-pedal

through currents.

Blinded in the haziness

of obscure idioms,

I stumbled, till a breeze,

so Wendy-like, gentle, yet forceful,

cleared the dull concepts,

enabling me to see

fallen leaves pirouetting

like little ballerinas.

And, behold, still waters at night,

reflecting a candle's flame.

And, from within the breeze,

I heard meaningful songs

in perfect meter,

beheld, above the wet,

her hand penning

its glassy surface

with a steady finger.

From a plain-worded embryo

deep inside poetry's womb,

fresh verses were conceived,

uttering burning songs

from the scattered ashes

of my penned obscurities. [37]

My Scholar

He stirred and blessed my pen,

when ineptness owned my heart and face.

O, Father, my Lord, my Friend,

I claimed each concept with Your grace.

A sanguine brew, just below the rim,

quenched my thirst,

a sip made me think,

flamed the dim wisdom,

aflame in my grip.

Comprehension rejoiced aloud,

vast teachings to be learned.

Come, hear His wee voice

in a crowd,

no beseeching,

Heavenly Scholar earned. [38]

My Pen

I make rainbows appear,
volcanoes erupt,
turn murky waters clear,
persuade clamor to hush,
warm freezing hearts,
declare all men friends,
and influence scholars' thoughts,
all with a stroke of MY PEN.
I chat with Socrates,
refute Einstein and Freud,
float upon a breeze,
enhance the image of God,
give roaming gypsies roots,
predict eternity's end,
bestow justice and truth
with the stroke of MY PEN.
I change frowns to smiles,
visit distant stars,
enlighten the beguiled,
touch dreams afar,
place wars under peace,
resurrect glee,
give hunger a feast,
proclaim God's victory.

Sickness is healed,
massive mountains thinned,
reveal ugliness' appeal,
with the stroke of MY PEN.
Melt Arctic icebergs,
trek distant galaxies,
sing merrily for each dirge,
make every man free,
converse with the dead,
create a compassionate blend,
extract fear from those afraid,
with the stroke of MY PEN.
I reflect God's grace,
dispel Satan's pollution,
give patience to haste,
provide just solutions,
arm love to conquer hate,
amend and amend,
alter wretched fates
with the stroke of MY PEN.
I can freeze Hell and all demons within,
for a power excels
with each stroke of MY PEN. [39]

One Day # 1

One day,

just to wake to all I must bear.

One day,

to break my unbroken nightmares.

This sweet, early rise,

sunshine kissing my face,

I seek tomorrow's eye,

anticipating her pace. [40]

(A simple and somewhat romantic way to describe the value of one day of life is this: We cannot embrace tomorrow without today. Oh, to be awakened by God's sweet kiss of life. Some people didn't wake up this morning! We should be grateful, but for some reason, being grateful for just waking up is often overlooked. Can you imagine being grateful, I mean, truly grateful, for waking each morning? Doing that changes your entire day Think about that.

I've been humoring you with Parenthesis, and I am he, but I am also Suddenly. Just be aware that it took forty-four years of prison, out of my sixty-four years of life, to suddenly appear to not be a curse to anyone but, rather, a blessing to everyone.

I'm really enjoying myself, sharing my thoughts and concepts. It's rare for me to do this.

Read on.)

Juba [41]

Bewildered, horded onto ships,

chained, lashed with whips,

defiled, yet clutching pride,

degraded and shamed,

despair staked its claim.

Juba, Juba and survive!

Stripped of language and name,

Kunta and Kizzi became John and Jane,

denied freedom of choice.

Odds defied each endeavor,

some shined cleaver.

Juba, Juba and rejoice!

---

41. For those who don't know, Dictionary.com defines *Juba* as: "a
  lively dance accompanied by rhythmic hand clapping, devel-
  oped by plantation slaves of the U.S." The name *Juba* derives
  from the capital and largest city of the South Sudan. Juba,
  then, is the Black man's way of escaping from his troubles.

168

A rhythmic glee of hand claps,

frenzied moves and thigh slaps,

a triumphant dance.

A smiling appearance of joy

concealed the annoyance.

Juba, Juba and advance!

All dat pickin' cotton has been forgotten.

New crops are in da fold.

Hatin' and killin' one another,

no respect for sistas and brothas.

Juba, Juba yet in our soul! [42]

Black Forest Legacy

Within the ghetto's dense forest,
from a hail of burning slugs raining down
in semi-auto succession,
saplings are obliterated.
Flesh gleams through crimson
oozing from jagged bark,
orbs, blinded by fate,
stare into nothingness,
as lost souls tap mercy's door.
And, when no one answers,
barge in on the neighboring darkness
(the door to Hell is always open).
Outward, beyond the threshold,
flowing in the veins of scions
born long after the suffering
of ancestors crowded
into the bellies of slave ships,
eyes, searching the dark,

for hope never beheld,
ears, filled with the sound of wailing,
nostrils swelling in the stench of filth
mingling with death.
Condemnation awaited survivors.
The legacy is forgotten,
and, somewhere, spirits are weeping,
their once mighty roots,
now vague in saplings
risen from a great culture.
Far beyond ideologies
of slingin' n blingin'
n flossin' n bein'
the numba one stunna
of these contemporary times,
the legacy lives only
as an old, obscure memory. [43]

(Black people, we need to remember the past to beautify the future. We were planted in fields of violence and abuse, but that doesn't mean we should be harvests of the same. We must destroy the unpleasantries of the past, not for our race, but for the world. We have endured! Let's strengthen the world. I'm about to flip the script. Check it out.)

Ode To a Ballerina

Dressed in a sequined tutu,
sparkling radiantly,
an enchanting ballerina,
staged for all eyes to see.
Rosy cheeks and a bonny smile,
beneath a shimmering crown,
her exquisite swan-like poise,
the audience, spellbound.
On masterfully pointed toes,
she took breathtaking leaps,
jete'd like spring pixies,
after winter's sleep.
A truly delicate idol,
intrigued with mystique,
arabesque, poised motionless,
a nimble stance before she peaked.
She pirouetted perfectly,
spinning like a magical top,
'round and 'round and 'round.
Seemed she would never stop.
Her reverence signaled the end
of a performance without flaw.
Claimed her bouquet of roses,
curtsied to the applause. [44]

(If you're wondering, I had to go to the prison library to gain a basic understanding of what a ballerina was all about.)

(From a distance, I used to listen to other guys in prison. Some of their stories of failure touched me. I wrote about some of them in poetic form.)

Guilty of Love

Years confined, no longer few,
days reflect desert sand,
time seemed to crawl but flew.
Now, silver crowns the man.
Each day inside of cubic Hell,
pleasant thoughts, unforsaken,
absorb the gloom of his cell,
bestows when he is shaken.
Thoughts of Delilah,
his once darling wife,
remained the same each dream.
Time has thwarted the loathsome tides.
True love has been redeemed.
For many a year, no mail bore his name.
Delilah, had long since said, "Goodbye,"
ousting ties without shame
to be the apple of another's eye.

Remembering Delilah's fair eyes'
glare for the luxuries of life,
fully aware, no love they'd share
without opulence for his wife.
An aging aunt's wealth, kept by stealth,
a secret always concealed.
But, tired of Delilah's whining pelts,
secrets were revealed.
Delilah began to strain
for the secret to gain,
a foolish scheme
caused his aunt to die.
But, in dying pain,
she scribbled the name of her nephew
to whom she confided.
Delilah testified on his behalf,
though the jury couldn't tell,
the way she smiled,
giggled and laughed,
booked his trip straight to Hell.
His love to hate, then hate to love,
she pared his penchant through time,
needing forgiveness from God above.
Being GUILTY OF LOVE was his crime. [45]

(Let's stop and chat for a moment. I like being Parenthesis. The concept of it is unique, but as it turns out, I am also Suddenly. Meeting Rev. Lady was the driving force behind this book. It's so much easier with her inspiration, motivation and encouragement. Suddenly we met, and this book is a chapter in the aftermath.

Now here's more of me.)

Katrina, the Bitch

(I am aware of the fact that the true meaning of the word *bitch* is a female dog, but there is a more common use of the word, and that is what I mean here.)

She was a bitch, a good for nothing one,

a cruel, destructive home-wrecker.

Just ask 'em down in N'awlins.

They'd agree wholeheartedly,

give freighting details

of her announced debut,

how she came, flirting,

on vicious Gulf winds

that raised her long, flowing dress,

exposed her devasting behind

to a gaping Big Easy.

On national TV,

she made Nagin swear,

Blanco weep,

and Bush less dignified.

Like I said, she was a bitch.

She dis' everyone,

had Forti's ganstas and thugs

feeling like victims,

stuck on the overpass,

saying silent prayers,

hoping a real God would hear

and answer them.

Yeah, she filled the Dome with chaos,

made FEMA stop pimping the public,

to become its personal trick.

She gave N'awlins a big wet kiss,

with lingering effects.

Yeah, she was a bitch,

'cause no lady would ever act that way. [46]

Deborah

Deborah, Deborah,
O, lovely Deborah,
apple of many an eye,
suddenly perplexed,
gentle spirit vexed,
broken, your will to survive.
Deborah, Deborah,
O, dearest Deborah,
by deception you were wrought,
pure maiden of a vow,
bestowed thyself somehow
chaste pledge equaled naught.
Deborah, Deborah,
O, sightless Deborah,
couldn't see his heart was vile,
the love of a fool
to a gigolo's rule,
left alone, awaiting child.
Deborah, Deborah,
O, saddened Deborah,
eyes, so full of tears,
defeat was nibbling,

no comfort from siblings,
contemplated the end near.
Deborah, Deborah,
O, bewildered Deborah,
life flowed through your veins.
His venomous fruit
planted seeds,
thus, sprouted roots,
created your deepest shame.
Deborah, Deborah,
O, bedamned Deborah,
on a high cliff,
above the sea,
took a wingless flight
into the dark of night,
drowning thy unborn and thee.
Deborah, Deborah,
O, farewell, Deborah,
in a coffin,
forever to sleep,
thy and thee alone,
a daughter, yet not born
are but sad memories to keep. [47]

(The guy this previous poem is about took his sister's suicide very hard. He had been the only sibling she could talk to, and he wasn't there for her when she needed him. I felt his pain. I deeply feel everything I write about. Come now, let's go on.)

Mary Lou

At one time, my dear,

tears were smeared

upon my saddened face.

Now, no grief remains,

all stains erased.

Behold, this boy, once coy,

found joy in a girl named Mary Lou.

For her splendid charms,

I flew into her arms.

The lady's rare and true.

You since see

she comforts me easily,

freely, with glee,

even if out of her way.

What happiness! Yes, and bliss!

The girl makes my day.

She makes no excuses,

constitutes no ruses

like you had me believe.

Oh, but what she does I love

because she never deceives.

So, go on talk and stalk,

I'll walk right past the childish scene.

'Cause, Girl, what we had was bad,

and I'm glad I'm with

the girl of my dreams.

You seem hurt, pert, without mirth,

and down in mood,

since I chose a rose that glows,

a rose named Mary Lou. [48]

Dreams Forgotten

Subconsciously piqued on reveries plain,

morning's falling drops of sugary rain,

and in dark, glowing apparitions

become vague

with confrontation.

Friendly spirits eclipse the nights'

many slumberous plights

of diluted realities,

"forbidden."

Awake, dreams hidden! [49]

A Twinkling Star

O, twinkling star against dark skies,

beyond my touch,

yet not too high,

thou does exist,

a distant truth.

I shall succeed,

reaching for you! [50]

Butterfly

Belated effects of deep remorse
created a metamorphosis,
rendering me compassionate.
Softened by time, my heart,
once a roaring lion,
now whispers like a butterfly,
searching a place to rest its wings.
A harmless butterfly
of colorful, symmetrical beauty
marred only by wormy memories
of a time before emerging
from a cocoon
to face a discarding world,
yet mindful of my wormy days.
Although, my colorful beauty
lies exact through my heart,
once upon a time,
I crawled. [51]

Born To Die

Whack!

An open palm,

a wailing debut,

the first cry.

Whack ...

disturbed the calm.

Tick-tock the clock.

BORN TO DIE.

Death be not the worst,

but rather to be denied

entrance into Heaven,

no mirth.

Salvation needed!

BORN TO DIE! [52]

Woman in My Dream

Appearing within my dream,

a bewitching, welcomed sight,

her presence in my space

unraveled lovelorn plights,

before she fled came morning's light.

With kisses upon my lips

shattering reality,

her raw femininity

piqued me excitingly.

Ah, such serenity

inside my reveries!

Within my dreams

her sparkle brightened

the darkened slumber,

hushed the screaming thunder

of my penal throes and woes,

thus, freed me, there yonder,

inside of my dreamy wonders.

In somnolence, I felt her,

a specter of conception

and romantic reflections.

Her love and charm

helps keep me warm

with sugared-down deception.

Her memory lingers

through hard daily chores.

Oh, why, did I wake,

this madness to partake?

Yet, hoping she smiles

when night breaks! [53]

Laws of Life

13,763 days,

thirty-eight years of existence.

I give God the praise

for His blessing of persistence

to conquer all resistance.

It's been a brain-strain,

trying to make a change.

Each harvest of pardons

are rooted in gardens

overseen by wardens.

The confirmation of this tangled situation

are lengthy vines of incarceration,

sprouting from toxic fertilizers

that make victims of victimizers,

through contrasting laws

with no regards for the blindfolded broad.

Got me seeking God.

I've tried everything else,

so, I began placing His commandments

under my belt:

Thou shall have no other God before Me.

Thou shall not worship a carved image or idol.

Thou shall not use the name

of Lord thy God in vain.

Remember the Sabbath.

Honor thy father and mother.

Thou shall not commit murder.

Thou shall not commit adultery.

Thou shall not steal.

Thou shall not bear false witness

against thy neighbor.

Thou shall not bear false witness

against thy neighbor's wife.

These are the LAWS OF LIFE,

but we've buried them deep,

sand beneath the sea.

And yet, because of the depth of vanity,

we know not glee.

Trying to mimic God's wrath. Why?

He was known to wage war.

So we fight for silly maters. Why?

Because our egos are fatter

than any spiritual realm,

thinking we're at the helm.

Within a blink, we could be abolished,

along with the knowledge

of thinking that we're "bout it-bout it."

Go ahead and laugh.

Truth is, we don't have many

1,300-day spans.

Man ain't sand,

and we're not going to be here forever.

Nah, that's a never-never!

Lord, help me get myself together.

I've tried everything else,

so I'm placing Your commandments

under my belt:

Thou shall have no other before me.

Thou shall not worship a carved image or idol.

Thou shall not use the name

of the LORD thy God in vain.

Remember the Sabbath.

Honor thy father and mother.

Thy shall not commit murder.

Thou shall not commit adultery.

Thou shall not steal.

Thou shall not bear false witness

against thy neighbor.

Thou shall not bear false witness

against thy neighbor's wife. [54]

These are the LAWS OF LIFE.

Smile

Once there was a Man

who died on a cross

to save the world from sin,

and every time I think

of how He sacrificed His life,

I SMILE. [55]

Another Day

I kiss the dark good night,
embrace each tomorrow
after praying to wake,
in spite of my joy, grief and sorrow.
When open my lids,
all inside each day, I claim,
though often, some, I try to rid,
I face all, without blame.
It is not about the troubles in life,
but, rather, life itself.
So, absorb calm as well as strife,
and store that span upon a shelf.
Count it as another blessing
for which you've paid the price,
just by living
ANOTHER DAY of life! [56]

(I may be regarded as somewhat poetic, but I need you to know that my poems are my true feelings for God and life. I'm just blessed with the ability of worded expressiveness. Reading my literature affords a path to feeling and understanding my heart.

Oh, God has been patient with me, and He still is. I must share these poems you. These concepts enabled me to endure more than four decades inside with joy in my heart. I had no chance of ever being free, and still I had joy in my heart. I did it one day at a time, hoping for tomorrow and knowing there was no guarantee. There is peace in living that way. There is even more time for God.

And SUDDENLY, I am.)

Darkness Abandoned

Enslaved, laboring on street corners

until Angola cradled me

in her surrogate arms.

It was d déjà vu,

having chosen confinement

long before she breast-fed me

inside of this barred crib

I have long since outgrown.

For many lonely years,

Angola's wretched dim

completely engulfed me.

Before my eyes adjusted

to behold the despair,

my ears were filled

with the clamor of rattling chains

echoing through narrow corridors.

Gradually, I beheld hazy visions

of hope mingling with madness.

I needed more.

I needed illumination

and found it in Bible verses.

At first, appearing so faint,

I thought it a hoax

created by my need

to walk beneath a shine,

yet the glint intrigued no less,

thus held me hostage.

Eventually, it's faintness became

a luminous wonder.

Now, despite confinement,

I am free from darkness. [57]

Deception

The lion tamer enters the lion's cage

with a flare,

brandishing a whip and chair,

fully aware, that his glare

of apparent control

comes only from patience.

The lion's vicious roar

sounds an understanding.

The tamer pretends to be demanding,

concealing the fact

that it's all an act,

a pact made to behave.

So, the tamer parades,

thrice as deceptive as brave! [58]

Mourn Not

Why, when someone dies,

do we mourn?

We should weep

for the child just born. [59]

59. Copyright © 2018 by Frederick Jones

Warehouse

Stowed away in a warehouse,
upon a crowded shelf,
is product #82382.
Upon this crowded shelf,
reality, barely visible under
the depleted rays of hope.
Upon this crowded shelf,
sunshine strokes somberly,
stars, rare delights,
each joyous effect of raindrops
reflect a memorable childhood glee.
And birds,
roaming in the sky,
are airborne wonders.
Upon this crowded shelf,
gulping the flowing madness,
while thrashing for far beyond.
Within this warehouse,
upon crowded shelves,
items are catalogued and stowed
to gather the dust of time! [60]

Devouring Joy

Often, I pen in woeful joy,

a tasteful flavor added

to the dull consumption

of this barred crib,

spicing the bland menu

of my daily routines.

Yes, I have been gluttonous.

Full, I, in the joy of scribing,

possess a child's sentiments,

a child surrounded by bubbles,

bursting them with glee.

With clarity, metaphors bestow upon me

a philosophical décor,

garnished and laced with truth.

Submerged in this madness,

penning, my DEVOURING JOY! [61]

(I never thought I'd share this much of me. I was writing a book of poetry, and reluctance overwhelmed me. Some of my work is very personal.
I have more.)

Journey

On the twisted path I chose to trek,
my full weight on a frail staff
caused it to break.
Thus, crawling became an act.
I learned to do it well.
From victimizer to victim,
contained by a vicious justice,
I became digitized.
My vague future manifested itself
from a foolish past.
Know, without promise,
tomorrow comes quickly,
yet uncertainty shall find me humbled,
simply waking each day.
And, should death come today,
it will greet me a better man
than he who began this JOURNEY. [62]

(Reverend Lady has given me the reigns, but like I said earlier, I am SUDDENLY, and living in the aftermath of our sudden encounter is a blessing that can only come from God. Hallelujah!

Let's go somewhere, God is awesome, and He has a master plan for everything. So, to stay on course, we must line up with His Word. We can't do that unless we believe there is a God. For over three decades, without accepting Jesus, I wrote godly things. I know now it was for a reason. I don't yet know what. I just know that God has work for me to do. Hopefully, in the process, I will be able to bless my home. More talk later.)

Survivor

Youthful	Violated
Confused	Pretended
Rebellious	Runaway
Thief	Robber
Captured	Pretended
Imprisoned	Paroled
Foolish	Robber
Caught	Imprisoned
Defiant	Weary
Penned	
Thinker	Penned
Reasoned	Penned
Remorseful	Penned
Motherless	Penned
Childless	
Penned	Fatherless
Penned	Strength
Aspired	Survivor [63]

Legend

When it comes to mortality,

death does not discriminate.

Thus, alive, I am a LEGEND.

Although, just a whisper,

my voice utters like great men before me,

men hushed by their mortal demise,

an end that serves everyone,

mocking the existence

of each passing second.

And, through every moment of life,

by His grace alone,

I am a LEGEND! [64]

Warrior

Fettered in a concrete garden,

I have tended iron flowers

with very gentle thoughts.

I have defeated time

by conquering seconds.

I have absorbed my mother's

once-broken heart,

beheld the mended cracks

until she died.

I have destroyed

my father's disappointments

to become one of his reasons

to smile before he died.

I have overcome abandoning my sons
to see them become good fathers.
I have subdued immaturity
by becoming responsible.
I have defeated scorn
with reasons for love.
I am a WARRIOR,
battling an army
of resisting force,
fighting, regardless of odds,
the enemy—ME! [65]

65. Copyright © 2018 by Frederick Jones

(I hope I have been more than interesting thus far. One thing's for sure: I had a ball with the Parenthesis concept. It was cool.
Through all my trials, God kept His hand on me. He freed me from the jaws of the beast, and He gave me Reverend Lady.)

Hilda: God didn't give me away. He blessed us with love for one another.

(Oh, the dead has risen!)

Hilda: Funny. You know I'm reading everything.

(Be my guest. I've been sharing my thoughts while you've been taking care of ministry business. I have no doubt that you will be pleased.)

Hilda: Stop!

(What?)

Hilda: You know you're trying to charm me.

Suddenly

(Darling, I wouldn't do that.)

Stop it! You're messing up my hair.

(Shh … ! More poetry?)

Mirage

In this desert, at a distance,

worldly concepts shimmer

like diamonds caressed by a radiant beam.

Hovering inevitably,

death, unpredictable, thrives,

though often ignored.

Deceiving ourselves, we yield not.

We forsake our living and loving God.

So swiftly, tomorrow comes a callin',

possessing the power

to purge the poison

from consumption

of worldly concepts. [66]

Eulogy

Here stands a man befitting his EULOGY.

Thirty-three years, a lifetime,

to experience a freshness,

after dying over and over,

resurrected each time,

only to die again.

What remains in him

are hazy, youthful memories

of a span time has absorbed.

Now, here he is,

grateful for his own demise,

at peace with himself,

yearning to roam. [67]

Love More Thyself

Each day you wake,

life, sparkling true,

should begin with God,

then, gradually, you.

There is no wrong

to LOVE MORE THYSELF,

Just make God first,

beyond all else.

Practice well, this simple chore

of loving God,

then thyself more. [68]

(Well, I've been running my mouth, or should I say, inking? Anyway, I have neglected saying a prayer. I hope I'm not offending anyone, but I need to say a prayer:

Our father who art in heaven, hallowed be thy name. Thy kingdom come. Thy will be done on earth as it is in heaven. Give us this day our daily bread and forgive us our trespasses as we forgive those who trespass against us. And lead us not into temptation, but deliver us from evil. For thine is the Kingdom and the power and the glory forever.   *AMEN!*

Lord,
So many times, we don't know what to ask You for, and we ask for the wrong things. Dear Lord, first, we want You to know that we are grateful for waking up this morning. Everything starts with waking up. Somebody didn't wake up this morning, so, Lord, we thank You for allowing us to continue hopes and dreams for life.

God, help us to draw closer to You. Bless us with Your presence. Fill us with Your Spirit. Teach us to love, dear Father. Teach us to love. Make the world aware of love's strength and power.

God, make us know that You are Love, and, thus, Jesus is LOVE.

God, help us not to be lost in worldly things, and enlighten us on the spiritual things that we know little of.

Lord, touch hearts and open eyes.

In Your Divine Son's name, Jesus.

Amen!

Hilda: That was a nice prayer. Very unselfish.

(Thanks!)

Hilda: Well, well, Suddenly, I thank God for my husband. Every day isn't all smiles, but we go through it together, and in love. Even when we disagree, we sleep close to each other. In the aftermath of suddenly meeting a man with a sentence of 198 years and falling in love with him, I am now happily married to him. Sometimes, he's not easy, with his concepts and reasoning, but I've learned (once, the hard way), that most of the time he's right. Still he doesn't have a wild ego. I'm married to a good man.

(It is a blessing to be your husband. Exhale, my love, share yourself with the world as it inhales. You are good, not perfect, but good, very good. God lives in your heart, and I know. I make room for Him every day. He's there when we sleep, when we laugh, we cry, or we're off in our own thoughts. Reverend Lady, I'm going to do the work necessary to make myself worthy of your love. Girl, I love me some you.)

Hilda: Yeah, we're happy. My marriage to Hank prepared me for Ricky. I know that a hundred and ninety-eight years is a lot of time, but I tell you, Ricky spoke his way out of that place. After a few weeks of prayer, he began making promises about being home for Christmas. And he wasn't the type of man to do that. When I tried to stop him from saying that, he didn't want to hear it. He told me that God had forgiven him and would set him free for

Christmas. He was sure of it! Glory to God! Hallelujah!

He had prayed for a few weeks, and God spoke to Him, and He knew that God was true to His word. So, he knew he would be free for Christmas. Sure enough, he was released from Angola Prison on December 4.

(It wasn't luck or good fortune. It was God, the God I spoke of in my poems. I had to go through forty years of prison, and it took thirty-eight of those years to meet Rev. Lady, my beloved wife. God kept me through it all.)

Hilda: Everyone's entitled to their own opinion. Ricky and I will continue to believe that God moved in our live and blessed us with each other. We may not have much, but just being together is joy for us. We're happy. And, we give God all the glory. Hallelujah!

(I have a couple more poems for you. Like most of my other poems, I wrote these long before I met Reverend Lady.)

Love Defined
in Questions

Does it comfort you
when I say, "I love you?"
Or when I display it?
Is my embrace comforting,
my kiss exciting?
When you say to me, "I love you,"
are you truly sure?
If you are, why?
Is it my character?
My spirit or my smile?
Or perhaps, my promise
of unconditional love?
Could it be for the fact that I cherish you
like a wilted leaf does the morning dew?
Do you love me because I make you feel good
or because you feel I am good for you?
Would you face adversity
to insure our togetherness?
Would you love me the same at my worst,
as if I were at my best?
Love is many questions.
Do you love me? [69]

Love, O Love

LOVE, O LOVE,

hate often tries to bind,

yet free you will always be,

for those seeking to find.

LOVE, O LOVE,

torn and soiled,

remedy to all that ails,

from you, why do they recoil?

LOVE, O LOVE,

whispers in the wind,

those with harkening heart's joy

will never end.

Jesus is Love!

Yes, it is true.

"Love and you will find Him,"

assures the Spirit inside of you. [70]

(For every ending there's a new beginning. Whether you know it or not, that's good news. It magnifies God's purpose for our lives. We won't be here always. One day it will end, and, thus, a new beginning. There's an option to Heaven, only one. Have a little talk with Jesus.

It seems, I am unable to stop, so, right here and now, I, Parenthesis, will compose a poem to commemorate our encounter.)

Parenthesis' Song for Eyes

Thoughts heal, wounds have bled,

words, truth-appealed,

as you've read.

We have laughed,

cried, lived, died,

tried and tried.

We've been nigh, yonder,

pondered and pondered

on things often overlooked.

Myself, I once took this precious life for granted.

Now, we need to get planted in the Word.

Ya heard me?

I say, Let not greed nor scorn

be your need, be your thorn.

When weary, and times are hard

don't get teary.

Call on God.

Seems like you're holding

all the wrong cards?

Stop gambling,

and call on God.

He gives grit when times are hard.

I insist, try a little God.

His darling Son, Jesus, receives us,

will never leave or deceive us.

Yeah, that's how He sees us.

I, Parenthesis, enjoyed myself.

Now, please store me

upon your mental shelf. [71]

Hilda: There are no goodbyes. Reader, allow me to pray with you:

Lord Jesus, I come in Your holy name, thanking You for Your mercy and grace. Through Your love and blessings, my husband and I were inspired to write this book. I thank You for the gift of knowledge and wisdom mingling with the experiences in this book. And, hopefully, someone facing adversity will be inspired to seek and trust You. Your Word declares:

Philippians 4:13

I can do all things through Christ which strengtheneth me.

Lord, let Your people know that You can do anything. It's all about You, Jesus, dying on that cross. Now, Lord Jesus, encourage Your people. Let them know that love has already conquered what threatens us.

Lord, bless Your people and meet their needs. Let them know that there is hope through Christ which strengthens even those with incarcerated loved ones. Open their eyes so that they may see that You are the answer.

And, Lord, touch the hearts of men and women in prisons. Inspire them to surrender their hearts and not their garments. Let the words in this book be planted in fertile soil. Lord, let it encourage Your people. Thank You, Lord, for Your mercy.

In Jesus' name,
Amen!

Only God

How dare you!
Who do you think you are?
You felt a deep remorse
for all the people you hurt
after you were caught
and sentenced to 198 years.
How dare you!
I am forgiven!
I did not repent to God.
I repented to myself,
vowed never to again hurt people
in thought nor action.
Sincerity swelled in my heart.
It wasn't till I met Reverend Lady,
that I was able to cry out to God
for His forgiveness.
Eighteen months later, I was free.
ONLY GOD knew my heart. [72]

(I hope it has been intriguing and delighting for you to share my poetic trials. My poems are very personal, yet they are enlightening, with the motivating possibility of helping someone through something. These were the thoughts that carried me through prison life, but let me remind you, I had cleansed my heart. May God bless and keep you. Perhaps we'll share again.)

The Beginning

About the Author

Pastor/Evangelist Hilda Miller-Jones is the daughter of the late Helen McCloud and the step-daughter of the late James A. McCloud. She was married to the late Rev. Henry L. Miller and then to Frederick "Ricky" Jones in 2016. She has four children, twenty-four grandchildren and seventeen great-grandchildren. She was born in New Orleans, Louisiana and raised in Braithwaite, Louisiana.

In March of 1978, she joined House of Deliverances Church, attending house-to-house services under the leadership of Apostle Mary Trask, Rev. Josephine Jenkins and Rev. Cornelius Trask. These three elders took Evangelist Miller-Jones under their wings, training and teaching her the Word of God. She was later called by God to preach and teach His Word.

In March of 2003, she received her ordination papers and became a licensed minister. In November of that year God touched the heart of Hank and Hilda to start Faith, Hope and Love Ministry. In 2015 she was ordained as a pastor.

Evangelist Miller-Jones is a certified counselor with Mending the Nets Ministry, Inc. and was chosen to represent Louisiana post Katrina evacuees in Brazos, Valley, Texas. While employed at Texas A&M College, she completed several clerical courses. Upon returning to New Orleans, her studies enabled her to become an Administrative Secretary in Pastoral Care.

She has ministered on KKNO 750 am and WVOG 600 am radio stations in New Orleans, on The Rock of Ages Ministries Telecast, Apostle Ronnie Bailey, Pray the Word, Say the Word Ministry, Dr. Rev Josie Phillips, Operation Outreach for Souls telecast with Dr. June B. Paul and currently hosts the Faith Hope Love weekly telecast on NOLA Cox 76.

Evangelist Miller-Jones has written this book because of the years of encouraging her husband, and other inmates and their families, that there is hope in Jesus Christ.

Author Contact Page

You may contact the authors in the following ways:

Hilda Miller-Jones
Faith, Hope and Love Ministries
eMail: faithhopelov01@gmail.com
Phone: 504-215-4423

Fred R. Ricks
eMail: ministerofsong01@gmail.com
Phone: 504-509-7736

www.ingramcontent.com/pod-product-compliance
Lightning Source LLC
Chambersburg PA
CBHW030923090426
42737CB00007B/302